ROOSEVELT AND CHURCHILL

A FRIENDSHIP THAT SAVED THE WORLD

AL CIMINO

CHARTWELL
BOOKS

CONTENTS

INTRODUCTION

The acquaintanceship between Franklin D. Roosevelt, 32nd President of the United States, and Winston Churchill, wartime Prime Minister of the United Kingdom, began with twenty years of stony silence. Then as the world faced the gravest peril it had ever known—the manic thirst for world domination by Adolf Hitler and Nazi Germany—Roosevelt and Churchill recognized each other as vital allies. Their urgent need for one another's support soon turned into a firm friendship. And when the US was brought into World War II by Hitler's ally, militarist Japan under General Hideki Tojo, their friendship became vital to each other's survival and the survival of their nations.

They were frequently in communication by telephone, telegram, and letter, and risked life and limb traveling in wartime to meet up with each other. Starting on September 11, 1939—a week after Britain and France declared war on Germany—and ending on April 11, 1945—the day before Roosevelt died—their correspondence comprised nearly two thousand letters and cables. They spent a hundred and thirty days together, including Christmas, New Year's, and Thanksgiving, in the White House, at Roosevelt's home at Hyde Park, at Shangri-La—later renamed Camp David by President Eisenhower—on various warships, on the presidential train, and at conferences in Casablanca, Quebec, Tehran, and Yalta. They had a brief holiday together in Marrakech, where Roosevelt was carried to the top of a tower so that he could see the winter sun setting over the snow-capped Atlas Mountains. Churchill later painted the scene for him. It was the only painting he completed during the war.

Thrown together in a war that consumed millions—the greatest single event of the

Franklin D. Roosevelt, 1933.

twentieth century—they were surrounded by politicians, generals, and aides who would write portraits of the relationship between Roosevelt and Churchill in their memoirs. The wives, children, and friends of the two men would also write their versions. And the two leaders gave their own account of the bond, both in public and in private.

Their friendship was rarely straightforward. They disagreed politically and shamelessly used each other to their own ends. But they still had the greatest affection and respect for each other. Often they would sit up late into the night drinking and smoking together, while less robust figures had long since retired.

Both men were fallible and, with the gift of hindsight, we can see that both made political and strategic mistakes—sometimes at the cost of thousands of lives. However, without their bond the war against Nazism, Fascism, and Japan's imperial ambitions would have been lost and freedom-loving nations would have been crushed under the yoke of these dark forces. Together they steered the world through the greatest danger it had ever known and emerged victorious. Theirs was indeed a friendship that saved the world.

Winston Churchill in Downing Street giving his famous V-for-Victory sign.

PART ONE

THE GUARDIANS OF FREEDOM

Being with them was like sitting between two lions roaring at the same time.

Mary Churchill, Winston Churchill's daughter

CHAPTER 1

THE DIE IS CAST

On Sunday, December 7, 1941, President Roosevelt was having lunch at his desk in the Oval Office with advisor Harry Hopkins. They were talking, Hopkins recalled, "about things far removed from the war" when the telephone rang. It was the Secretary of the Navy Frank Knox who told Roosevelt that a radio message had been picked up from Hawaii saying that the US Pacific Fleet's base there, Pearl Harbor, was under attack from an air raid and this was "no drill." Hopkins expressed disbelief, but Roosevelt said he thought it was "just the unexpected sort of thing the Japanese would do."

Some fifty minutes later Admiral Harold Stark, Chief of Naval Operations, confirmed that there has been an attack, severe damage had been done and there had been some loss of life. By 3 p.m., Roosevelt had convened a meeting of Knox, Stark, Secretary of War Henry L. Stimson, Secretary of State Cordell Hull, and US Army Chief of Staff General George C. Marshall. Hopkins recalled:

> The conference met in not too tense an atmosphere because I think that all of us believed that in the last analysis the enemy was Hitler and that he could never be defeated without force of arms; that sooner or later we were bound to be in the war and that Japan has given us an opportunity. Everyone, however, agreed on the seriousness of the war and that it would be a long, hard struggle.

TIRED AND DEPRESSED

That Sunday, Winston Churchill was at Chequers, the British Prime Minister's country residence. His guests included the American Ambassador John Gilbert "Gil" Winant, Roosevelt's special envoy to Europe Averell Harriman, Churchill's Chief of Staff Major General Hastings Ismay, and Churchill's daughter-in-law Pamela.

Churchill was tired and depressed during dinner, lost in thought, and sometimes holding his head in his hands. Britain had been at war for three years. All of Western Europe had fallen to the Nazis. Invasion had been thwarted by the Battle of Britain, but that had only led to the devastation of the country's cities by bombing in the Blitz. There had been setbacks in the Mediterranean and North Africa. Hitler had turned his military power on the Soviet Union that June, but Stalin might turn out to be as much a liability as an ally.

Shortly before 9 p.m. Churchill's valet, Sawyers, brought in a portable radio so they could listen to the news. Churchill was a bit slow at switching it on and they missed the headlines. The first item the dinner party heard was about a tank battle in Libya.

Then the announcer returned to the lead story—that Japanese aircraft had attacked Pearl Harbor. Roosevelt had made an announcement, but the details of the attack were still sketchy. There was some argument among the diners at Chequers over whether the attack had been made on Pearl Harbor or the Pearl River.

Suddenly energized, Churchill slammed the top of the radio down, switching it off. Sawyers re-entered the room. "It's quite true," he said. "We heard it ourselves outside. The Japanese have attacked the Americans."

Confirmation came from the British Admiralty. Churchill headed for the door, saying: "We shall declare war on Japan."

Chasing after him, Winant said: "Good God, you can't declare war on a radio announcement."

IN THE SAME BOAT NOW

Winant phoned Roosevelt to confirm the facts and said he was with a friend who wanted to speak to him, adding: "You will know who it is as soon as you hear his voice."

"Mr. President," said Churchill, taking the phone. "What's this about Japan?"

"It's quite true," replied Roosevelt. "They have attacked us at Pearl Harbor. We are all in the same boat now."

"This certainly simplifies things," said Churchill. "God be with you."

"To have the United States on our side was to me the greatest joy," Churchill wrote later.

For seventeen months since the fall of France, Britain and its empire had fought on alone. Now, with America onboard, Churchill believed that the war could be won. He wrote:

> *The United States is like a gigantic boiler. Once the fire is lighted under it there is no limit to the power it can generate. Being saturated and satiated with emotion and sensation, I went to bed and slept the sleep of the saved and thankful.*

Roosevelt was not so sanguine. America would now be plunged into the war against Germany as well as one with Japan. He told his wife Eleanor:

> *I never wanted to fight this war on two fronts. We haven't got the Navy to fight in both the Atlantic and the Pacific ... so we will have to build up the Navy and the Air Force and that will mean that we will have to take a good many defeats before we can have a victory.*

FALSEHOODS AND DISTORTIONS

As more information came in from Hawaii, it was soon clear that aircraft from the Japanese Imperial Fleet had attacked Pearl Harbor, the US naval base at Oahu, Hawaii, and had sunk four American battleships of the Pacific Fleet, damaging four more. Nine other ships were destroyed or damaged along with more than three hundred aircraft, and over 2,400 people had been killed.

An hour after the attack, the Japanese Ambassador and Special Envoy arrived at the State Department with Tokyo's response to a US ultimatum of November 26. It accused the US of conspiring with Britain to prevent Japan creating a New Order in the Far East. It regretted that "the peace of the Pacific through cooperation ... has finally been lost" and ended by saying that it was now "impossible to reach an agreement through further negotiations." Even this was not a clear declaration of war. Reading the Japanese government's reply, Secretary of State Cordell Hull said:

> *In all my fifty years of public service I have never seen a document that was more crowded with infamous falsehoods and distortions, infamous falsehoods and distortions on a scale so huge that I never imagined until today that any government on this planet was capable of uttering them.*

The Japanese delegates apologized that the diplomatic note had been delivered an hour late because of problems decoding it. In fact, US codebreakers had already cracked it, but it had not specified where the attack would be. Hull had the reply all ready, having received a phone call telling him that Pearl Harbor was under attack before the Japanese delegation turned up.

President Roosevelt signing the declaration of war on Japan, December 8, 1941, the day following Japan's surprise attack on Pearl Harbor.

AVERELL HARRIMAN

Born in New York City, William Averell Harriman (1891 – 1986) was the son of railroad baron Edward Henry Harriman. After graduating from Yale, he went into railroads and banking using money inherited from his father. Later his sister encouraged him to join her and her friends the Roosevelts, working on the New Deal. He joined the National Recovery Administration and, later, the National Defense Advisory Commission, which then became the Office of Production Management.

In the spring of 1941, Roosevelt made him special envoy to Europe to help coordinate the Lend-Lease program. He was at the Atlantic Conference and traveled with Churchill to visit Stalin in Moscow in the summer of 1942. He also attended the conferences at Tehran, Yalta, and Potsdam.

From 1943 to 1946, Harriman served as US Ambassador to the Soviet Union, the Secretary of Commerce, and US representative to the European Recovery program. He ran unsuccessfully twice for the Democratic nomination for the presidency and served one term as governor of New York. Returning to diplomacy under Presidents John F. Kennedy and Lyndon B. Johnson, he served as the first head of the US delegation to the Paris peace talks which sought to bring an end to the Vietnam war.

In 1971, he married Pamela Churchill Hayward (1920 – 97), the former wife of Winston Churchill's son Randolph. In 1993, she became the 58th United States Ambassador to France. Harriman died on July 26, 1986, in Yorktown Heights, New York, at the age of 94.

HARRY L. HOPKINS

Born in Sioux City, Iowa, Henry "Harry" Lloyd Hopkins (1890 – 1946) moved to New York City after graduating in 1912 and became a social worker. Rejected for the draft in World War I because of a bad eye, he worked for the American Red Cross in New Orleans, returning to New York and social work in 1922. After the Wall Street Crash of 1929, Hopkins went to work for the Temporary Emergency Relief Fund set up by Roosevelt, then governor of New York. When Roosevelt became president in 1933, Hopkins moved to Washington DC as head of the Federal Emergency Relief Administration.

In 1938 he became Secretary of Commerce, but stomach cancer put an end to Hopkins' political ambitions. Nevertheless, he remained a trusted confidant. On May 10, 1940, after a long discussion about the German invasion of the Low Countries, Roosevelt urged a tired Hopkins to stay the night in a second-floor bedroom in the White House. Hopkins lived there for the next three-and-a-half years, continuing in residence even after marrying Louise Gill Macy in the Yellow Oval Room and only leaving at her insistence in December 1943.

He became Roosevelt's unofficial emissary to Winston Churchill, first visiting the British Prime Minister in January 1941 to assess Britain's prospects after the fall of France and the Battle of Britain. He was put in charge of the Lend-Lease program where the US gave or loaned weaponry to Allied nations in exchange for leases on army and naval bases in Allied territories. This was extended to the Soviet Union after Hitler attacked the USSR in June 1941. Hopkins went to Moscow to meet Joseph Stalin the following month.

Hopkins accompanied Churchill to meet FDR at the Atlantic Conference in Placentia Bay, Newfoundland, and attended the meetings at Cairo, Tehran, Casablanca, and Yalta. When Roosevelt died, he tried to resign due to his own declining health, but President Harry S. Truman sent him on one more mission to Moscow to help arrange the Potsdam Conference. After he died, there were repeated allegations that he was a Soviet agent. However, the evidence is thin.

A DATE WHICH WILL LIVE IN INFAMY

On December 8, President Roosevelt addressed a joint session of Congress, saying:

Yesterday, December 7, 1941—a date which will live in infamy—the United States of America was suddenly and deliberately attacked by naval and air forces of the Empire of Japan.

He pointed out that the attack had taken place while diplomatic dialogue was still going on and concluded by saying:

I ask that Congress declare that, since the unprovoked and dastardly attack by Japan on Sunday, December 7, a state of war has existed between the United States and the Japanese Empire.

The Senate passed the resolution by 82 to 0; the House of Representatives by 388 to 1—with only Representative Jeanette Rankin of Montana, who had also voted against US entry into World War I, opposing. And at 4:10 that afternoon, President Roosevelt signed the declaration of war. That same day, Britain, whose colonies in Malaya and Hong Kong had been attacked, also declared war on Japan. In accordance with the Tripartite Pact signed with Japan on September 1940, Germany and Italy declared war on the United States. And the US declared war on Germany and Italy. The die was now cast.

WAR PLAN

While Roosevelt was making his speech to Congress, Churchill was making plans to visit him. "We could review the whole war plan in light of reality and new facts," Churchill wrote. Roosevelt expressed concern that Churchill would be crossing an ocean that was full of German U-boats. When Churchill waved these concerns aside, Roosevelt said: "Delighted to have you here at the White House."

The scene of devastation at Pearl Harbor after the Japanese attack on December 7, 1941.

Leaving England four days later, Churchill arrived onboard the *Duke of York* in Norfolk, Virginia, on December 22, then he was flown on a US Navy plane the 140 miles to Washington. The President greeted him at the airport. Roosevelt had not even told his wife that Churchill was coming. That morning the White House butler, Alonzo Fields, had walked in on an argument.

"You should have told me!" said Eleanor. "If I had only known."

Roosevelt reassured her that Churchill would only be staying for "a few days." He ended up staying three weeks. Roosevelt simply instructed Fields that there would be twenty for dinner.

"It had not occurred to him," Eleanor observed in her syndicated column, "that this might require certain moving of furniture to adapt rooms to the purposes for which the Prime Minister wished to use them."

CHILD–LIKE IMPATIENCE

In fact, Roosevelt had not expected Churchill to arrive until the following day. The original schedule was that, after ten days at sea, the *Duke of York* would anchor in Chesapeake Bay, then cruise up the Potomac River to Washington, but Churchill's doctor Charles Wilson said:

He was like a child in his impatience to meet the President. He spoke as if every minute counted. It was absurd to waste time; he must fly.

Nevertheless, Eleanor offered the prime minister and his aides tea. Churchill had with him Minister of Supply Lord Beaverbrook, Dr. Wilson, technical staff, and Navy chieftains.

That night, over dinner, Roosevelt and Churchill exchanged jokes and anecdotes, while others retired to the Blue Room to discuss the war. The second-floor Rose Suite was turned into a mini-headquarters for the British government, with messengers carrying documents to and from their embassy in red leather cases. In the Monroe Room, where the First Lady usually held press conferences, they hung up large maps showing the progress of the war. They were not a happy sight, with Germany and Italy controlling Europe from the English Channel to the Black Sea, Hitler besieging Leningrad, and the Japanese sweeping through the Philippines and British Malaya. Hong Kong surrendered on Christmas Day.

Churchill was nothing if not demanding, telling Alonzo Fields:

I must have a tumbler of sherry in my room before breakfast, a couple of glasses of scotch and soda before lunch and French champagne, and ninety-year-old brandy before I go to sleep at night.

For breakfast, he asked for fruit, orange juice, a pot of tea, along with "something hot" and "something cold," which the White House kitchen interpreted as eggs on toast with bacon and two slices of cold meat with English mustard.

COCKTAILS IN THE RED ROOM

White House staff were in for a shock. They often saw the prime minister in his nightclothes, a silk gown with a Chinese dragon on it or one of his one-piece siren suits (a onesie of the time), often in lurid colors.

"We live here as a big family in the greatest intimacy and informality," Churchill wrote to Deputy Prime Minister Clement Attlee. Churchill was happy to take hold of Roosevelt's wheelchair and push him into the White House dining room.

They ate lunch together at Roosevelt's desk in the Oval Office every day. In mid-afternoon, Churchill would often retreat for a two-hour nap. He worked mostly after dinner, long into the night. He kept Roosevelt up until 2 or 3 a.m. drinking brandy, smoking cigars, and ignoring Eleanor's exasperation.

"It was astonishing to me that anyone could smoke so much and drink so much and keep perfectly well," she wrote. But it was in those late-night drinking sessions that they bonded.

Actually, Churchill was not drinking as much as she thought. Mixing drinks was one of the few physical things that Roosevelt could do easily in public. In what he called "children's hour", he would make cocktails in the Red Room.

"At cocktail time everything was beautifully stage-managed so that he could be in control, despite his disability," wrote Churchill's youngest daughter Mary.

He would be wheeled in and then spin around to be at the drinks table, where he could reach everything. There were the bottles, there was the shaker, there was the ice. It was all beautifully done. There was never an effort or scurry. He loved the ceremony of making the drinks; it was rather like, "Look, I can do it." It was formidable. And you knew you were supposed to just hand him your glass, and not reach for anything else. It was a lovely performance.

COMPLETELY VICTORIAN

Roosevelt called these drinks martinis, but they were experimental concoctions of vermouth, fruit juice, and gin, though rum from the Virgin Islands was sometimes substituted. Churchill could not stand cocktails of any variety, but the diplomacy of the situation obliged him to accept what the President handed him. Five minutes later, he would excuse himself and head for the bathroom, where he poured the drink down the toilet. Commenting on America after he left the White House, Churchill said: "The problem with this country is the drinks are too hard and the toilet paper's too soft."

Nevertheless, Churchill was a formidable drinker, though no one ever saw him drunk. Roosevelt did not even try to compete, but his cocktail hour was sacred.

Prime Minister Winston Churchill and President Franklin D. Roosevelt during a press conference in Washington, December 23, 1941.

Eleanor did not approve of heavy drinking. Her father had died of alcoholism when she was just ten and she was appalled at Churchill's behavior.

"The President did not share his wife's shock, nor her barely concealed disapproval," Nigel Hamilton wrote in *The Mantle of Command: FDR at War, 1941–1942.* "He liked eccentricity, which made people the more interesting." Churchill amused Roosevelt. "Winston is not Mid-Victorian—he is completely Victorian," Roosevelt said.

STATESMEN AND SHOWMEN

The day after Churchill arrived, Roosevelt introduced him to a hundred American reporters at a press conference on December 23. Harry Hopkins lounged in a window seat, while the reporters were checked by the Secret Service. Roosevelt leaned over to Churchill and remarked, *sotto voce,* that they were checking to make sure that no wolves in sheep's clothing entered.

Introducing Churchill, Roosevelt said: "He is quite willing to take on a conference, because we have one characteristic in common. We like new experiences in life."

The *Washington Star* said the atmosphere was "electric" and noted how much they were enjoying the occasion. The paper said:

Two great statesmen-showmen, sharing the star parts in a world drama that will be read and studied for centuries to come, played a sparkling and unique scene at the White House yesterday. They were President Roosevelt, debonair and facile as usual, and Britain's Prime Minister Churchill, jaunty and ruddy.

Roosevelt then asked Churchill, who was just 5 feet 6 inches tall, to stand up so that everyone could see him. The newsmen then cheered as the Prime Minister clambered up onto his chair and waved his cigar. He was "somewhat shorter than many expected," *The New York Times* reported, "but with confidence and determination written on the countenance so familiar to the world."

Churchill then batted back the journalist's questions with characteristic panache. Roosevelt was delighted. *Newsweek* wrote:

The smiling president looked like an old trouper who, on turning impresario, has produced a hit. And some thought they detected in his face admiration for a man who had at least equaled him in the part in which he himself was a star.

PINK AND WHITE ALL OVER

That evening, over dinner, they discussed the Boer War, the British campaign in 1899 – 1902 against settlers of Dutch and German descent in South Africa. At Harvard, Roosevelt had backed the Boers, while Churchill had been in South Africa in a British uniform and had returned a hero. Another guest said that the President was in a buoyant mood that evening and kept needling the Prime Minister.

"When he felt crowded too far, Churchill would take a puff on his cigar and counter attack with a verbal sally and then settle back again into his chair," he said.

However there were also signs of a growing friendship. A rueful Roosevelt admitted being a disappointment at Harvard. Churchill growled: "When I hear a man say that his childhood is the happiest time of his life, I think … my friend, you have had a pretty poor life."

Indeed, Roosevelt got to know Churchill even more intimately. Visiting his suite, Roosevelt knocked on the door and Churchill barked: "Come in."

Roosevelt entered to find Churchill, freshly emerged from the bath, pacing about stark naked, dictating correspondence to his assistant Patrick Kinna. Roosevelt apologized and retreated, but not before Churchill could gleefully announce: "You see Mr. President, I have nothing to hide from you."

Roosevelt later chuckled about it with his secretary Grace Tully, saying: "You know, Grace. I just happened to think of it now. He's pink and white all over."

Franklin D. Roosevelt campaigning to become
President of the United States, 1932.

CHAPTER 2

THE MASTERS OF OUR FATE

On Christmas Eve, 1941, Churchill joined the president at the annual White House Christmas tree lighting, which moved from Lafayette Park to the White House's South Portico due to wartime security considerations. In his address, Roosevelt said:

> *We have joined with many other Nations and peoples in a very great cause. Millions of them have been engaged in the task of defending good with their life-blood for months and for years. One of their great leaders stands beside me. He and his people in many parts of the world are having their Christmas trees with their little children around them, just as we do here. He and his people have pointed the way in courage and in sacrifice for the sake of little children everywhere. And so I am asking my associate, my old and good friend, to say a word to the people of America, old and young, tonight—Winston Churchill, Prime Minister of Great Britain.*

Churchill responded in kind, saying:

> *I spend this anniversary and festival far from my country, far from my family, yet I cannot truthfully say that I feel far from home. Whether it be the ties of blood on my mother's side, or the friendships I have developed here over many years of active life, or the commanding sentiment of comradeship in the common cause of great peoples who speak the same language, who kneel at the same altars and, to a very large extent, pursue the same ideals, I cannot feel myself a stranger here in the center and at the summit of the United States. I feel a sense of unity and fraternal association which, added to the kindliness of your welcome, convinces me that I have a right to sit at your fireside and share your Christmas joys.*

On Christmas Day Churchill attended a service with Roosevelt at a nearby Foundry Methodist Church. This was something that Roosevelt did not normally do. "I can do almost everything in the 'Goldfish Bowl' of the President's life," he said, "but I'll be hanged if I can say my prayers in it."

For Roosevelt, it was a poignant occasion. There were lilies on the altar in memory of his mother, who had died that September.

CONTENT TO LISTEN

The business of the war had to go on. It was agreed there should be a Combined Chiefs of Staff Committee in Washington to coordinate the Allied strategy. Charles Wilson noted:

> *For the first time I have seen Winston content to listen. You could almost feel the importance he attaches to bringing the President along with him, and in that good cause he has become a very model of restraint and self-discipline; it is surely a new Winston who is sitting there quite silent. And when he does say anything it is always something likely to fall pleasantly on the President's ear.*

Churchill spent most of Christmas Day working on the speech he would deliver the next day to a joint session of Congress. During cocktail hour, Churchill read a Biblical quote that he intended to use; Roosevelt liked it. There were sixty for dinner. Roosevelt had invited a number of cousins and friends. The President recalled in his toast to Britain that King George VI and Queen Elizabeth had dined in the same room in 1939, which he said marked "a beginning of the coming together of the two English-speaking races, which would go on after the war."

Franklin Roosevelt and Winston Churchill at the White House, Christmas 1941.

Churchill sat silent and preoccupied throughout the meal. After watching a newsreel, he excused himself, deciding against watching the film adaptation of *Oliver Twist*, saying: "I must prepare for tomorrow."

CHURCHILL'S SPEECH AT THE CAPITOL

Roosevelt wished Churchill good luck when he left for the Capitol the next day. Harry Hopkins was worried that the isolationist Congress might not be a very receptive audience for the man who had been urging America to join the war for three years now and had finally got his way. Roosevelt listened to the speech on the radio.

It was a triumph. He spoke of the honor it was to address them and wished his mother had been there to see it.

"I cannot help reflecting that if my father had been American and my mother British instead of the other way around, I might have got here on my own," he said.

He had come to Washington to meet the President to map out their military plans, he said:

Some people may be startled or momentarily depressed when, like your President, I speak of a long and a hard war. Our peoples would rather know the truth, somber though it be. And after all, when we are doing the noblest work in the world, not only defending our hearths and homes, but the cause of freedom in every land, the question of whether deliverance comes in 1942 or 1943 or 1944, falls into its proper place in the grand proportions of human history. Sure I am that this day, now, we are the masters of our fate. That the task which has been set is not above our strength. That its pangs and toils are not beyond our endurance.

The speech lasted for half-an-hour. At the end of it, he made a V-sign. The *Washington Post* said: "The effect was instantaneous, electric. The cheers swelled to a roar ... and fingers spread in the victory sign were raised in scores of places throughout the chamber."

When he got back to the White House excited and relieved, Roosevelt "told me I had done quite well," Churchill said. That evening, they watched *The Maltese Falcon* with Canadian Prime Minister Mackenzie King. Churchill said that the ending, where Humphrey Bogart's Sam Spade gives up the femme fatale he loves to the police, reminded him of a case he had handled as Home Secretary.

In his suite, Churchill got up during the night to open a window and was struck by a pain in his chest. He had had a minor heart attack. Dr. Wilson, not wanting to alarm him, simply told him he'd been overtaxing himself. Churchill, undaunted, took the train to Ottawa to address the Canadian parliament, then returned to Washington to continue the summit.

A JOINT DECLARATION

On New Year's Day 1942, Roosevelt and Churchill went to church together again, then visited Mount Vernon to lay a wreath on George Washington's tomb. Over dinner they discussed the Allied declaration that was going to be signed that evening. The pact included a historic new phrase. Roosevelt suggested a new name for the Allies—the United Nations. According to aide Harry Hopkins, Roosevelt hit upon the name that morning and wheeled himself to Churchill's suite, unannounced, to run it by the prime minister. Ignoring a clerk's warning that Churchill was in the bath, Roosevelt asked him to open the door. He did, revealing Churchill again standing naked on the bath mat. "Don't mind me," Roosevelt quipped.

The Soviet ambassador objected to a reference to religious freedom, preferring "freedom of conscience." Roosevelt convinced him that "religion" and "conscience" were the same thing as religious freedom gave the individual the right not to believe in God at all. Churchill was so impressed by Roosevelt's theological arguments that he offered to make him Archbishop of Canterbury if he lost the new presidential election. Later Churchill noted: "I did not however make any official recommendation to the Cabinet or the Crown upon this point, and as he won the election in 1944 it did not arise."

That night, they were to gather in the president's study with diplomats from several Allied countries to sign the joint declaration saying that they would fight the Axis powers together, and that none would negotiate a separate peace.

A STAB IN THE BACK

Those who sat next to Churchill at dinner complained that, no matter how far apart they were sitting, all Churchill's conversation was directed at Roosevelt. He took no interest in anyone else, even Mackenzie King who had been Churchill's principal ally up to that point.

When Roosevelt recalled the "Stab in the Back" speech he had made at the University of Virginia on June 10, 1940—the day Italy declared war on Britain and France—he said that the State Department had insisted he remove the phrase "the hand that held the dagger has struck it into the back of its neighbor" from the text. But on the way to the university, he had put it back in again. Churchill said he knew how he felt. He was always having to take things out of his speeches.

The President then said that the best thing to do with Hitler "would be to put him on a ship from which he would disappear." The talk turned to Hitler's failure to reach Moscow before the winter set in that year.

At the War Office in 1919, Churchill had supported the Allied intervention into Russia to "strangle Bolshevism in its cradle," which had been halted at Tula, just south of Moscow. However, Churchill said, he now forgave "the Russians in proportion to the number of Huns they killed."

In light of the new alliance between Britain and the Soviet Union, Harry Hopkins asked: "Do they forgive you?"

"In proportion to the number of tanks I send," Churchill replied.

Roosevelt and Churchill then adjourned to the Oval Office to sign the declaration, followed by the Soviet and Chinese envoys.

ARCADIA CONFERENCE

During Churchill's stay in Washington, there were a number of meetings between Churchill and Roosevelt, and their staff, code named Arcadia. In it, Roosevelt agreed to maintain the "Europe first" principle—that is, the US should concentrate its efforts on defeating Nazi Germany and Fascist Italy, while maintaining holding operations against Japan in the Pacific. There should be a build-up of forces in Britain in preparation for an invasion of France. There should also be a landing of US troops on the Atlantic coast of Morocco, behind the lines of the German forces the British were attacking out of Egypt. During the Arcadia Conference the wording of the Declaration of the United Nations was worked out, making a collective statement of the Allies' war aims as a sequel to the Atlantic Charter signed in Placentia Bay, Newfoundland, in 1940.

The United Nations Fight For Freedom— World War II propaganda poster.

DECLARATION BY UNITED NATIONS
JANUARY 1, 1942

A JOINT DECLARATION BY THE UNITED STATES OF AMERICA, THE UNITED KINGDOM OF GREAT BRITAIN AND NORTHERN IRELAND, THE UNION OF SOVIET SOCIALIST REPUBLICS, CHINA, AUSTRALIA, BELGIUM, CANADA, COSTA RICA, CUBA, CZECHOSLOVAKIA, DOMINICAN REPUBLIC, EL SALVADOR, GREECE, GUATEMALA, HAITI, HONDURAS, INDIA, LUXEMBOURG, NETHERLANDS, NEW ZEALAND, NICARAGUA, NORWAY, PANAMA, POLAND, SOUTH AFRICA, YUGOSLAVIA.

The Governments signatory hereto,

Having subscribed to a common program of purposes and principles embodied in the Joint Declaration of the President of the United States of America and the Prime Minister of Great Britain dated August 14, 1941, known as the Atlantic Charter.

Being convinced that complete victory over their enemies is essential to defend life, liberty, independence and religious freedom, and to preserve human rights and justice in their own lands as well as in other lands, and that they are now engaged in a common struggle against savage and brutal forces seeking to subjugate the world,

DECLARE:

(1) Each Government pledges itself to employ its full resources, military or economic, against those members of the Tripartite Pact and its adherents with which such government is at war.

(2) Each Government pledges itself to cooperate with the Governments signatory hereto and not to make a separate armistice or peace with the enemies.

The foregoing declaration may be adhered to by other nations which are, or which may be, rendering material assistance and contributions in the struggle for victory over Hitlerism.

There was a look of satisfaction on Churchill's face. Britain had for so long been on its own. Now, Churchill said, "four-fifths of the human race" were on their side.

Speechwriter Robert E. Sherwood summed up the relationship between the two great men:

> It would be an exaggeration to say that Roosevelt and Churchill became chums at this or any subsequent time. They established an easy intimacy, a joking informality and a moratorium on pomposity and cant—and also a degree of frankness in intercourse which, if not quite complete, was remarkably close to it … They were two men in the same line of business—politico-military leadership on a global scale—and theirs was a very limited field and the few who achieve it seldom have opportunities for getting together with fellow craftsmen in the same trade to compare notes and talk shop.

STATE OF THE UNION

Roosevelt's State of the Union speech followed on January 6. His staff were worried that Churchill's triumph on Capitol Hill would upstage their boss. "Roosevelt was not troubled; he was greatly amused by his friends' concern," Robert Sherwood said. Churchill was flattered when Roosevelt read a draft to him. In it, he said:

> Mr. Churchill and I understand each other, our motives and our purposes. Together, during the past two weeks, we have faced squarely the major military and economic problems of this greatest world war. All in our Nation have been cheered by Mr. Churchill's visit. We have been deeply stirred by his great message to us. He is welcome in our midst, and we unite in wishing him a safe return to his home. For we are fighting on the same side with the British people, who fought alone for long, terrible months, and withstood the enemy with fortitude and tenacity and skill.

Roosevelt was equally effusive behind Churchill's back. After New York Supreme Court Justice Sam Rosenman dined privately with Roosevelt, he said: "The conversation was mostly about Churchill—Roosevelt was most enthusiastic about him and praised his rugged, bold approach to the problems of war."

President Roosevelt delivering his State of the Union address to both houses of Congress, 1942.

However, working with Churchill was wearing Roosevelt out. "He laughingly remarked that he was looking forward to the Prime Minister's departure in order to get some sleep," said Rosenman. First Lady Eleanor Roosevelt also confirmed the extra stress Churchill caused:

> The prime minister took a long nap every afternoon, so was refreshed for hard work

> *in the evening and far into the night. While he was sleeping, Franklin had to catch up on all of his regular work. Even after Franklin finally retired, if important dispatches or messages came in, he was awakened no matter what the hour, and nearly every meal he was called on the telephone for some urgent matter. It always took him several days to catch up on sleep after Mr. Churchill left.*

CHURCHILL UNCOVERED

In Florida Churchill stayed in Lend-Lease administrator Edward Stettinius's house near Palm Beach where he splashed about naked in the surf. His doctor, Charles Wilson, described him as "half-submerged in the water like a hippopotamus in a swamp." His bodyguard Inspector Thompson tried to persuade him to wear bathing trunks. Churchill complained that no one knew he was there, the beach was secluded, and the sea was right outside the backdoor. When Thompson pointed out that he could be observed through binoculars, Churchill said: "If they are that much interested it is their own fault what they see."

Churchill was in a similar state of dishabille when his son Randolph visited him on May 18, 1940, while on leave from military training. His father was in front of the mirror, shaving in a silk undershirt. "It was the only thing he would wear to sleep in, and it left nothing to the imagination," his grandson later recalled.

In his biography of his father, Randolph recounted the scene. His father had told him to sit down and read the papers while he finished shaving:

> *I did as told. After two or three minutes of hacking away, he half turned and said: "I think I see my way through." He resumed his shaving. I was astounded, and said: "Do you mean that we can avoid defeat?" (which seemed credible) or "beat the bastards?" (which seemed incredible).*

> *He flung his Valet razor in to the basin, swung around, and said—"Of course I mean we can beat them."*

> *Me: "Well, I'm all for it, but I don't see how you can do it."*

> *By this time he had dried and sponged his face and turning round to me, said with great intensity: "I shall drag the United States in."*

Winston Churchill and his son Randolph, 1930.

A SERIOUS GAFFE

Churchill took a five-day vacation in Florida, during which he made a serious gaffe. He wanted to speak to Wendell Willkie who had quit the Democrats to run, unsuccessfully, as a Republican against Roosevelt in the 1940 presidential election. Seeing Willkie as the American equivalent of the British Leader of the Opposition, Churchill tried to call him, but the operator put him through to the Oval Office by mistake. Not only did Roosevelt discover that Churchill was going behind his back to contact his political rival, Churchill had not even recognized the voice until Roosevelt pointed out who he was.

Churchill was mortified, thinking his mistake might have alienated Roosevelt. Nevertheless, he could still joke with the President. When his vacation was over, Churchill phoned Roosevelt to tell him he was coming back to Washington. Bearing in mind that he had been warned about loose talk over insecure telephone lines, Churchill said: "I can't tell you how we are coming, but we are coming by puff-puff, got it? Puff-puff."

When he got back to Washington, Churchill consulted Harry Hopkins about the Willkie mix up and was reassured that no damage had been done.

DINNER AT THE WHITE HOUSE

Perhaps to annoy Churchill, Eleanor Roosevelt invited author Louis Adamic and his wife Stella to dinner on the penultimate night of his stay. Adamic had written a book called *Two-Way Passage*, which was fiercely anti-British and recommended US hegemony in Europe after the war. Churchill had read it and hated it.

Later Adamic would write a memoir of the evening called *Dinner at the White House*. In it he contrasted, Roosevelt—"fit, self-possessed, relaxed"—with Churchill—"rotund, dumpy

Franklin D. Roosevelt riding in a 1938 Cadillac during the 1940 campaign with bodyguards on the running board.

… a semi-scowl on his big, chubby, pink-and-white face."

"Hello, Winston," Roosevelt said as his guest entered.

"Evening, Mr. President," Churchill said, though he was less deferential in private.

"They were obviously friends, but—perhaps less obviously—friends of a special kind, in whose relations the personal and the supra-personal were turbulently mingled," Adamic said.

When Roosevelt asked whether he had had a good nap, Churchill "scowled … or perhaps 'pouted' is the more accurate word and sticking his cigar in his mouth, mumbled something neither Stella nor I understood, although the room was very still."

Roosevelt offered Churchill a cocktail.

"What are they?" Churchill asked.

"Orange blossoms."

Adamic said: "Churchill made a face, but he accepted the cocktail and drank it dutifully." When they went down to dinner, Churchill rode in the elevator with Roosevelt. Adamic noted that Eleanor delayed the other guests on the stairs, discussing the portraits that hung there. This, he surmised, was to give Roosevelt time to be wheeled into the dining room and transferred from his wheelchair to a seat at the table.

Another guest, Roosevelt's seventeen-year-old goddaughter Margaret Hambley, said that, over dinner, Churchill complained about how terrible it was of Hitler to "bomb all the beautiful scotch whisky and cigar warehouses. He said he didn't know what would happen to a country when its supplies of whisky and cigars ran out."

Churchill and Roosevelt then told the tale of how a box of Cuban cigars had been sent to Churchill as a Christmas present, only to find, when it was opened, it was full of worms. This made Hambley feel quite ill, which itself amused Churchill.

"He seemed to delight in my illness and went into more and more detail of how they crept through each cigar," she said.

WE FORGOT ZOG!

Other topics of conversation included religion in Germany, Hitler's foreign minister Joachim von Ribbentrop, college reunions, King Carol of Romania … Then someone asked about King Zog of Albania. Roosevelt cried out in surprise: "Zog!" Adamic recalled:

> The upper part of his body leapt up so that he almost seemed to rise. We all looked at him. He leaned over the table and pointed a finger at Churchill:
>
> "Winston, we forgot Zog!"
>
> Churchill puckered his lips as if to say: So what, or, as he probably would have put it: Well?…
>
> "Albania is a belligerent on our side," said the President. He scratched his head. "I believe there's an Albanian Minister or representative here—we must get him to sign our little document."

The other guests laughed, but Adamic, a Slovene, was offended. "A couple of emperors!" Adamic said to himself. "Says one emperor to the other across the dinner table: 'Oh, say, we forgot Zog.' It's funny as hell. But too damned personal, haphazard, high-handed, casual. What else have they overlooked?"

Churchill got his own back on Adamic. In 1947, he sued the author after he had added a footnote saying that Churchill's policy toward Greece had been influenced by his obligations to Hambros Bank. In an out-of-court settlement, Churchill received substantial damages.

BRANDY AND CIGARS

After dinner, the Adamics went to a concert with Eleanor, leaving Churchill and Roosevelt chatting and joking. Roosevelt had insisted that Hambley and her school friend Anne Curzon-Howe stay to keep them company, possibly as an antidote to the sober and serious Adamics.

"I don't think FDR was happy that they were there when Churchill was," said Hambley.

"FDR and Churchill relaxed after they left."

Churchill and Anne discovered that they were distantly related through the Curzon family and he insisted that she call him "Cousin Winston."

Then the question of age came up.

"The P.M. said that a woman was as old as she looked; a man was as old as he felt; and a boy was as old as he was treated," Margaret Hambley recalled. Churchill appeared downcast. "You know I must be the oldest man ever to have been in the White House." No, no, Roosevelt interjected. "The Pres. said there had been someone 95 there, so he cheered up."

Clearly, the two men were in their element.

"Brandy and the usual cigars were going strong," Anne Curzon-Howe noted, "and W. and FDR seemed to be getting on famously and capping each other's stories."

SINGLE COMMAND CENTER

Serious work was done too. During the visit, Churchill and Roosevelt agreed on several strategies that would end up being fruitful for the war effort. Churchill learned to his relief that, despite America's impatience for revenge on the Japanese, Roosevelt still intended to defeat Germany first, as the two leaders agreed when they first met five months earlier. They also agreed that the US would join the British fighting the Axis in North Africa later that year. Landings there would prove an effective prelude to the Allied assault on Italy and France.

At Roosevelt's insistence, Churchill agreed that there would be a single command center in Washington where supreme Allied commanders in Europe and Asia would coordinate the war effort. This deeply upset British military leaders, but Churchill headed off criticism by telegraphing Attlee, the acting prime minister in his absence, that it was a done deal.

TRUST ME TO THE BITTER END

On Churchill's last evening in Washington, he dined along with Roosevelt and Harry Hopkins. There was still paperwork to do. Churchill was to sign a copy of the first volume of his book *The River War*, his account of fighting in Sudan in 1899, for his host. His inscription read: *Inscribed for President Franklin D. Roosevelt by Winston S. Churchill. In rough times January 1942.*

Churchill lingered an hour beyond his scheduled departure time. Roosevelt's last words to him were: "Trust me, to the bitter end."

The Prime Minister flew home via Bermuda on January 14, 1942, carrying a letter from Hopkins to Churchill's wife Clementine. In it, Hopkins had written:

> *You would have been quite proud of your husband on this trip. First because he was ever so good-natured. I didn't see him take anybody's head off and he eats and drinks with his customary vigor and still dislikes the same people. If he had half as good a time here as the President did in having him about the White House he surely will carry pleasant memories of the past three weeks.*

LATE NIGHTS TAKE A TOLL

Pleasant memories or not, the meeting of the two leaders was seen to be crucial. "His visit to the United States has marked a turning-point of the war," said *The Times* of London of Churchill's visit. "No praise can be too high for the far-sightedness and promptness of the decision to make it."

Late nights with Churchill had taken a toll on Roosevelt and exhausted his staff. Hopkins checked himself into the naval hospital to recover. But the bond between President and Prime Minister—a trust that would win the war—had been forged. Roosevelt, in the now-quiet White House, found he missed Churchill's company. He sent a message to him in London, saying simply: "It is fun to be in same decade with you."

CHAPTER 3

AN UNLIKELY ALLIANCE

On March 18, 1945, with victory in sight, Churchill told Roosevelt: "Our friendship is the rock on which I build for the future of the world." Though fortuitous, it was a very unlikely friendship, Roosevelt and Churchill were such very different characters. While their friendship was forged in war, their war aims were very different. Churchill sought to preserve the British Empire, which he had served his entire adult life. Roosevelt wanted to liberate colonized peoples—whether the colonizing power was Germany or Britain, Japan or France or the Netherlands.

Churchill came to power as a war leader in 1940, known for his belligerence, while Roosevelt had been re-elected in 1940, promising to keep the US out of the war. Churchill had been in and out of wars all his life—in India, the Sudan, South Africa, and the trenches of France in World War I. Roosevelt was wheelchair-bound and had only observed war from afar.

Churchill was spontaneous and warm. Roosevelt was distant and wily. "He is the coldest man I have ever met," said his third Vice-President and successor Harry Truman. "He didn't give a damn personally for me or you or anyone else in the world as far as I could see. But he was a great president."

PRIVILEGED BACKGROUNDS

There were similarities too. Both loved liquor, tobacco, the sea, battleships, politics, power, and the sound of their own voices. Together they steered the world through the greatest danger it had ever known and emerged victorious.

Although they were both from privileged backgrounds, their upbringings were very different. They had been born eight years apart—Franklin Delano Roosevelt at Hyde Park in Dutchess County, upstate New York, on January 30, 1882; Winston Leonard Spencer-Churchill at Blenheim Palace, Oxfordshire, England, on November 30, 1874. Both had rich American mothers.

In 1880 Roosevelt's mother, Sara Delano, whose own father made his fortune in the opium trade in China, became the second wife of James Roosevelt, whose money came from coal and railroads. Churchill's mother Jennie Jerome, daughter of a prosperous New York financier, married Lord Randolph Churchill, a prominent British politician, in 1874. Young Roosevelt also had a politician in the family—Theodore Roosevelt, who was US president from 1901 to 1909 and a Republican, was a distant cousin.

Theodore Roosevelt (1858 – 1919) was the 26th President of the United States, 1901 – 1909.

REVEREND ENDICOTT PEABODY

Endicott Peabody (1857 – 1944) was an Episcopal priest who founded Groton. He took the young Roosevelt under his wing and passed on the preaching of Victorian cleric, the Reverend Frederick W. Robertson, who said: "We will not say much of the wretchedness of doubt. To believe is to be strong. Doubt cramps energy. Belief is power. Only so far as a man believes strongly and mightily, can he act cheerfully, or do anything that is worth doing."

In 1934, Roosevelt said: "As long as I live his influence will mean more to me than that of any other people next to my father and mother."

He even cited Peabody in his last inaugural address, saying:

> I remember that my old schoolmaster, Dr. Peabody, said in days that seemed to us then to be secure and untroubled, "Things in life will not always run smoothly. Sometimes we will be rising toward the heights—then all will seem to reverse itself and start downward. The great fact to remember is that the trend of civilization itself is forever upward; that a line drawn through the middle of the peaks and the valleys of the centuries always has an upward trend."

Another loyal alumnus of Groton was future Secretary of State Dean Acheson. When the Rector visited him in 1939, Acheson remarked that Britain needed both Churchill and Peabody. The Rector replied that his British friends did not think that Churchill was enough of a gentleman to which Acheson, comparing Churchill to the courteous pre-war British Prime Minster, Neville Chamberlain, said: "Chamberlain doesn't understand what he is up against, but he would be a great success as a student at Groton. Churchill does understand it. He would have been kicked out of Groton in a week."

ELEANOR ROOSEVELT

Born Anna Eleanor Roosevelt (1884 – 1962) in New York City, she was the daughter of Elliott Roosevelt, the younger brother of Teddy and Roosevelt's godfather. He was an alcoholic who was often forbidden to see her. Eleanor's mother was the beautiful but distant Anna Hall, who called her daughter "granny" because of her old-fashioned looks. Both her parents were dead by the time she was ten. Her maternal grandmother sent her to school in England. When she returned to New York, she taught at a settlement house on the Lower East Side.

She and Roosevelt had known each other slightly as children. After a chance meeting he began courting her. She feared that he was so handsome and she so plain that he would not stay in love with her for long. President Theodore Roosevelt gave her away at her wedding. Between 1906 and 1916 they had six children, one of whom died in infancy.

Roosevelt's mother Sara tried to dominate her son's married life. She played the matriarch at Hyde Park and they had adjoining houses with connecting doors in New York. When he became a state senator in 1911, they moved to Albany where Eleanor took on the role of a political wife. She continued in that role in Washington, when he became Assistant Secretary of the Navy.

In 1918, she discovered that he was having an affair with her social secretary, Lucy Mercer. For the sake of his political career, he agreed to stop seeing Mercer, rather than divorce. But he was not good to his word and continued to meet Mercer regularly. Indeed she was with him on the day he died in 1945. Meanwhile Eleanor loyally continued to help his political career, acting as his eyes and ears after he was paralyzed by polio.

She worked as a teacher and became an activist in her own right, lobbying particularly for African Americans, the poor, and the young. As First Lady she began writing her "My Day" syndicated column six days a week, which she continued until she died.

After Roosevelt died, President Truman appointed her as a US delegate to the United Nations General Assembly. There she served as chair of the Commission on Human Rights and had a major hand in the drafting of the Universal Declaration of Human Rights of 1948.

Both boys were dedicated collectors. Roosevelt amassed books, birds, stamps, and naval prints; Churchill toy soldiers and butterflies. They both loved movies and read the same books—Shakespeare, Macaulay, Kipling, Edward Lear, and tales of derring-do.

A PAMPERED CHILDHOOD

As a child Roosevelt was pampered. He had a Swiss tutor who taught him at home. His summers were spent touring Europe. At age 14, he was sent to Groton, a boarding school in Massachusetts. In 1900, he entered Harvard, where he studied sparingly in favor of his social life. He became president of the student newspaper, *The Crimson*, and affected the mannerisms of Theodore Roosevelt, who was then president. However, he was blackballed by the most exclusive of the Harvard "final clubs," the Porcellian, to which both his father and cousin Theodore had belonged. It was, he said, "the greatest disappointment in my life."

COUSIN ELEANOR

While Roosevelt was at Harvard, his father died and his mother moved to Boston to be near her son. He idolized his mother and would commemorate the day of his father's death for the rest of his life. By the time he graduated, Roosevelt was secretly engaged to his fifth cousin and Theodore Roosevelt's niece Eleanor, who was then involved in charitable work for the poor in New York City. When his mother discovered this, she insisted that they wait for a year before they got married. Meanwhile she took Roosevelt away on a cruise. But he was not to be dissuaded. Roosevelt and Eleanor married in 1905. By then he was a student at Columbia Law School. He worked as a legal clerk.

EXPLOITING A REPUBLICAN SPLIT

His cousin Theodore Roosevelt was urging young men of privileged backgrounds to enter public service. Roosevelt's chance came in 1910, when the leaders of the Democratic Party in Dutchess County, NY, invited him to run for the state senate. The race seemed hopeless, but by exploiting a split in the Republican Party and denouncing the New York City Democratic political machine Tammany Hall, Roosevelt won.

He supported progressive New Jersey governor Woodrow Wilson for the Democratic presidential nomination of 1912. When Wilson entered the White House, he offered Roosevelt the post of Assistant Secretary of the Navy, a position Theodore Roosevelt had used to launch his national political career fifteen years earlier.

Franklin Delano Roosevelt in 1893, at the age of 11.

A DISDAINED SOCIAL WASTREL

While Roosevelt had been cosseted as a child, Churchill had been disdained. His father was stern and distant; his mother neglectful, devoting much of her time to her numerous lovers. He was largely brought up by his nanny Mrs. Everest who he called "Woom" or "Woomany." When she visited him at his boarding school, Harrow, he walked arm in arm with her up the High Street while other boys jeered. Later, when she fell fatally ill, he rushed to her bedside, afterward arranging her funeral.

He did not do well at school. Much to his father's disgust he entered the lowest class possible at Harrow and stayed there three times as long as any other boys had. Clearly he was not cut out for university and only passed the entrance exam to the Royal Military College (now Academy) at Sandhurst on the third attempt. His marks were so low that his father wrote to him threatening to break off all contact "if you cannot prevent yourself from leading the idle useless unprofitable life you have had during your schooldays and later months you will become a mere social wastrel, one of the hundreds of the public school failures."

THE WARRIOR HEROES OF THE PAST

Being put in the lowest class at Harrow, Churchill was spared learning Latin and Greek. Instead, he could concentrate on studying English. Some sixty years after leaving school, he won the Nobel Prize for Literature.

A teacher named Parkin interested him in the great heroes of British history—in particular Admiral Horatio Nelson who repeatedly defeated the naval forces of French dictator Napoleon Bonaparte. Churchill remembered Mr. Parkin's lessons:

> He told us how at Trafalgar Nelson's signal—"England expects that every man this day will do his duty"—ran down the line of battle, and how if we and our Colonies all held together, a day would come when such a signal would run not merely along a line of ships, but along a line of nations.

It was a lesson not to be wasted. After HMS *Cossack* rescued 290 captured British seamen from a sunken German raider, Churchill told an audience at London's Guildhall on February 23, 1940:

> The warrior heroes of the past may look down, as Nelson's monument looks down upon us now, without any feeling that the island race has lost its daring or that the examples which they set in bygone centuries have faded as the generations have succeeded to one another ... And to Nelson's immortal signal of 135 years ago, "England expects that every man will do his duty," there may now be added last week's no less proud reply, "The Navy is here."

Winston Churchill as a Harrow schoolboy in 1889.

A GOOD DAY TO DIE

Churchill's entry to Sandhurst was delayed following an accident that resulted in a ruptured kidney. During his long recuperation he went to the House of Commons at every opportunity. He did well at Royal Military College and graduated twentieth in a class of 130. During his final year, he courted public controversy for the first time. When the moral reformers organized a campaign to exclude prostitutes from the bar of the Empire Theatre in London's Leicester Square, Churchill incited some of his fellow cadets to riot and pull down the screens which had been put up to separate prostitutes from theatergoers.

"Ladies of the Empire," Churchill declared in an impromptu speech, "I stand for Liberty!"

Shortly before he passed out from Sandhurst in 1895, his father died at age 45 after a long decline. Like Roosevelt, Churchill commemorated the day of his father's death for the rest of his life. In the 1950s, he said to his private secretary Jock Colville: "Today is the twenty-fourth of January. It is the day my father died. It is the day that I shall die too." Strangely enough Churchill indeed died on January 24, 1965.

READY FOR ADVENTURE

The early death of his father left Churchill eager to make his mark. He obtained a commission in the Queen's Own Hussars. Before joining his regiment in India, he went to cover the Cuban war of independence from Spanish rule for the *Daily Graphic*, visiting New York en route.

In India Churchill spent his time reading in a voracious program of self-education—studying, among other things, parliamentary debates. He also saw action as a soldier and journalist on the North-West Frontier, turning his dispatches into the book *The Story of the Malakand Field Force*. He followed that with the novel *Savrola*.

Ready for adventure, he obtained a posting to the expeditionary force in Sudan, taking part in the British Army's last cavalry charge in the Battle of Omdurman, where his regiment galloped by accident into a ravine full of armed Dervishes. Churchill shot and killed at least three of the enemy with his Mauser pistol, and was lucky to survive the hand-to-hand fighting in which twenty-two British officers and men were killed.

Charge of the 21st Lancers at the Battle of Omdurman, Sudan, 1898, in which Winston Churchill took part.

"Another fifty or sixty casualties would have made our performance historic," he wrote to his mother, "and made us proud of our race and our blood."

He turned his dispatches from the Sudan for the *Morning Post* into *The River War*. In it, he showed a remarkable sympathy for the enemy, writing:

> *Those whose practice it is to regard their own nation as possessing a monopoly of virtue and common sense are wont to ascribe every military enterprise of savage people to fanaticism. They calmly ignore obvious and legitimate motives ... upon the whole there exists no better case for rebellion than presented itself to the Sudanese.*

BRITAIN'S CIVILIZING MISSION

Churchill was also critical of the British commander Lord Kitchener for his part in the desecration of the Mahdi's tomb and the slaughter of wounded Dervish soldiers.

Nevertheless, he continued to believe in Britain's "civilizing mission" in Africa and Asia.

Resigning his commission, Churchill headed for South Africa to cover the Boer War for the *Morning Post*. A journalist who traveled with him wrote: "I had not before encountered this sort of ambition, unabashed, frankly egotistical, communicating its excitement, and extorting sympathy."

Not content merely to report on the war, he joined the action and was captured. He escaped single-handed, making his way via Portuguese East Africa, now Mozambique, to return to Durban a hero. Over the objections of the war office, he joined his cousin Charles "Sunny" Spencer-Churchill, 9th Duke of Marlborough, in the thick of the fighting, fortified by regular supplies from Fortnum & Mason. These adventures supplied material for two more books. Writing not only gave Churchill a wonderful opportunity for self-promotion, but he also supported himself with his pen throughout his life.

As a war correspondent for the *Morning Post*, Winston Churchill (standing on the right) was captured by the Boers during the Second Anglo-Boer War in South Africa, 1899.

Lady Henrietta Blanche Ogilvy, the mother of Clementine Churchill (1885 – 1977), was notoriously promiscuous and Clementine came to believe that her mother's husband, Colonel Henry Montague Hozier, was not her father. Her parents separated when she was six. A debutante known for her beauty, charm, and intelligence, she first met Churchill in 1904.

Awkward around beautiful women, Churchill was dumbstruck. She was secretly engaged twice until she met him again at a dinner party in 1908, marrying him soon after. She was 23, he ten years older. They had five children.

Throughout their married life, Clementine fretted about his love of danger and the often perilous state of his finances. She designed his one-piece siren suits, known in the family as "rompers." They were often made in exotic shades of velvet. Generally he was an infuriating man to live with, unexpectedly returning home with a bunch of fellow politicians and expecting her to lay on lavish meals at a moment's notice. They often argued—once she threw a dish of spinach at him, which missed—but they soon made up.

In the 1930s, Clementine traveled around the Dutch East Indies aboard Lord Moyne's yacht the *Rosaura*, without Churchill. During this trip she had an affair with Terence Philip, a wealthy art dealer seven years her junior. Returning to her husband, she dismissed this liaison as "a holiday romance." She remained Churchill's confidante and his greatest supporter, sharing his belief that it was his destiny to lead Britain to victory in World War II.

Once Churchill confided to Roosevelt that he told Clemmie everything.

"I don't do that with Eleanor," Roosevelt replied, "because she writes a column and she might confuse what should be said and what shouldn't be."

Churchill was equally indiscreet in front of the children, then warned them: "Now that's secret." As they were hardly likely to run off and tell the newspaper, they would sometimes be offended by this. If he sensed they were upset, he would say: "It isn't that I don't trust you, but I'm labeling it."

MEMBER OF PARLIAMENT

In 1899, Churchill stood as Conservative Party candidate in a by-election in Oldham, but was beaten. At the general election the following year, he stood again, this time successfully. But before the next sitting of parliament, he made a lucrative lecture tour of the UK, US, and Canada with a magic lantern show of his escape from the Boers.

While in the US in 1900, Churchill met Theodore Roosevelt who was not unimpressed: "I saw the Englishman, Winston Churchill here, and although he is not an attractive fellow, I was interested in some of the things he said."

When he read Churchill's biography of his father *Lord Randolph Churchill*, Teddy Roosevelt was at best equivocal, saying:

I have been over Winston Churchill's life of his father. I dislike the father and dislike the son, so I may be prejudiced. Still, I feel that, while the biographer and his subject possess some real far-sightedness … they possess or possest such levity, lack of sobriety, lack of permanent principle and an inordinate thirst for that cheap form of admiration which is given to notoriety, as to make them poor public servants.

Elsewhere Roosevelt dismissed the book as a "clever, forceful, rather cheap and vulgar life of that clever, forceful, rather cheap and vulgar egoist, his father." And he told his son: "I can't help feeling about both of them that the older one was a rather cheap character, and the younger one is a rather cheap character."

In his maiden speech in the House of Commons on February 18, 1901, Churchill lent his strong support to the war effort in South Africa, though again he showed sympathy for the enemy, saying: "If I were a Boer I hope I should be fighting in the field."

CROSSING THE FLOOR

Although Churchill was the offspring of the landed aristocracy, he mixed with plutocrats. When the pioneering socialist Beatrice Webb first met him in 1903, she said he was "egotistical, bumptious, shallow-minded and reactionary, but with a certain personal magnetism, great pluck and some originality, not of intellect but of character. More of the American speculator than the English aristocrat."

After arguing with the Conservative Party over free trade, Churchill crossed the floor of the House, taking his seat on the Liberal benches beside David Lloyd George. At the time, he was still writing the biography of his father, who he portrayed as a Tory with radical sympathies.

When the Liberals formed a minority government, Churchill became under-secretary at the Colonial Office, seizing the opportunity to tour Britain's African possessions, while getting a series of articles and a book out of it.

Theodore Roosevelt read *My African Journey* which was serialized in *The Strand Magazine* and liked it. He wrote to the US Ambassador in London, Whitelaw Reid, saying: "I do not like Winston Churchill but I supposed I ought to write him. Will you send him the enclosed letter if it is all right?" The letter read:

My dear Mr. Churchill: Thru Mr. Reid I have just received the beautiful copy of your book, and I wish to thank you for it. I had read all the chapters as they came out, with a great deal of interest; not only the chapters upon the very important and difficult problems of the Government itself, but also the hunting chapters and especially the one describing how you got that rare and valuable trophy, a white rhinoceros head. Everyone has been most kind to me about my proposed trip to Africa. I trust I shall have as good luck as you had.

In the subsequent 1906 general election the Liberals won a landslide victory and Churchill was elected MP for Manchester North West. He joined the Cabinet as president of the Board of Trade and, after losing his Manchester seat in 1908, took the safe Liberal seat of Dundee in Scotland in a by-election which he retained until 1922. After his proposal to American actress Ethel Barrymore was rejected, he married Clementine Hozier.

CHAPTER 4

ALLIES AGAINST FASCISM

During his time in Parliament, Churchill worked closely with David Lloyd George, though he was very much the junior partner. Daughter of Prime Minister Herbert Asquith and later author of a memoir about Churchill, Violet Bonham Carter said:

> *His was the only personal leadership I have ever known Winston to accept unquestioningly in the whole of his career. He was fascinated by a mind more swift and agile than his own ... From Lloyd George he was to learn the language of Radicalism.*

Together they promoted radical reforms, though opposed socialism. "Socialism seeks to pull down wealth," Churchill said in 1908. "Liberalism seeks to raise up poverty ... Socialism would kill enterprise; Liberalism would rescue enterprise from the trammels of privilege and preference."

BEING HOME SECRETARY

In January 1910, Churchill became Home Secretary, where he continued his program of social reforms, though he suffered opprobrium for the heavy-handed policing of suffragette rallies and strikes. Teddy Roosevelt attended the funeral of Edward VII in 1910 and said: "I have refused to meet Winston Churchill, being able to avoid any scandal by doing so. All the other public men, on both sides, I was glad to meet."

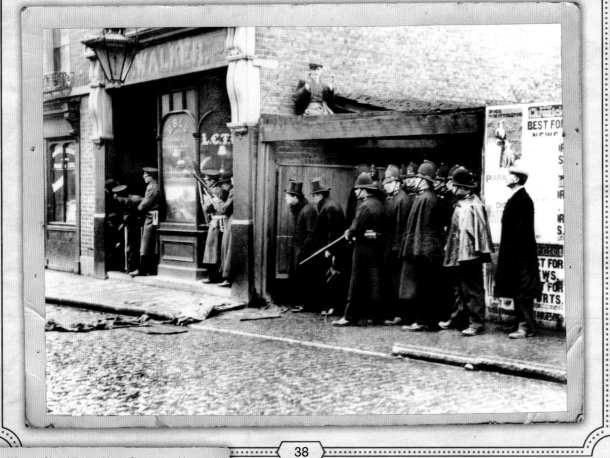

Winston Churchill, then Home Secretary, with armed police in Sidney Street, East London, January 1911.

After a bungled jewel robbery where three policemen were killed, a gang of Russian anarchists were cornered in a house in Sidney Street in the East End of London and shots were exchanged. Churchill rushed to the scene and was captured in the danger zone by a newsreel camera. He gave permission for troops to be called in and, when the house caught fire, approved the decision to let it burn down, killing those inside.

JOINING THE ADMIRALTY

In October 1911, Churchill was transferred to the Admiralty where he sought to maintain the Royal Navy's superiority over the burgeoning German Fleet, converting coal-fired ships to oil and encouraging the development of submarines and air power—even taking flying lessons himself, until Clementine persuaded him to stop. He also sought a naval alliance with France.

When World War I began, Churchill was determined to play a part in the fighting on land as well as at sea, turning the naval reserve into the Royal Naval division, a fighting force of 15,000 infantrymen. He also had three squadrons of Royal Navy planes bombing German defenses from airfields in northern France.

When the Western Front became deadlocked he championed the development of the tank. His industry even impressed Theodore Roosevelt, who wrote to an English friend:

I have never liked Winston Churchill but in view of what you tell me as to his admirable conduct and nerve in mobilizing the fleet, I do wish that if it comes your way you would extend to him my congratulations on his action.

THE DARDANELLES DISASTER

As First Lord of the Admiralty, Churchill also put himself in the way of danger, on the ground organizing the defense of Antwerp with his Royal Naval division, helping the

THE HOUSE OF COMMONS

Churchill had a great love of the House of Commons, an institution that in wartime as well as peace could make or break him at any time. On March 5, 1917, back-bench Liberal MP Alexander MacCallum Scott recalled:

As we were leaving the House late tonight, he [Churchill] called me into the Chamber to take a last look round. All was darkness except a ring of faint light all around under the gallery. We could dimly see the table, but walls and roof were invisible. "Look at it," he said. "This little place is what makes the difference between us and Germany. It is in virtue of this that we shall muddle through to success and for lack of this Germany's brilliant efficiency leads her to final disaster. This little room is the shrine of the world's liberties."

Belgian Army to escape. In another attempt to break the stalemate on the Western Front, he backed the campaign to force a passage into the Black Sea through the Dardanelles straits, a narrow 60-mile-long strip of water that divides Europe from Asia. The aim was to take the pressure off the Russian Army fighting against Germany on the Eastern Front and shorten the war.

However, due to poor leadership, the Allied Force got held up during an attempted military landing on the Gallipoli peninsula in April 1915. Bombarded by the fierce Turkish defenses, every attempt to land was defeated, incurring heavy casualties. By mid-January 1916, all the Allied troops were withdrawn and the attack on the Dardanelles was abandoned.

The Liberal government was replaced by a coalition. Churchill took the blame and was forced to resign. To overcome the depression this brought on, Churchill took up oil-painting. The Dardanelles campaign remains to this day one of the most controversial episodes of World War I.

In January 1916, he took command of the 6th Battalion of the Royal Scots Fusiliers on the Western Front. He was frequently under fire and had a number of narrow escapes from death. After a hundred days at the front, his battalion was merged with another one, extinguishing his command. He resigned his commission. A committee investigating the Dardanelles campaign absolved him of responsibility for its failure, allowing him to return to politics.

TWO WAYS BEGINNING WITH A

In July 1917, Lloyd George, now Prime Minister, appointed Churchill Minister of Munitions, over the complaints of Tory MPs and the Conservative press. Lloyd George only managed to square the appointment with the coalition partners by keeping Churchill out of the War Cabinet. In this role, Churchill made frequent trips to France and concluded: "There are only two ways left now of winning the war, and they both begin with A. One is aeroplanes and the other is America."

Churchill worked closely with Bernard Baruch, who was chairman of President Wilson's War Industries Board. Baruch later worked on Roosevelt's New Deal and, when the US entered World War II, he was special advisor to the director of the Office of War Mobilization and subsequently became head of the War Production Board, again having privileged contact with Churchill.

In April 1918, Churchill suggested that the Allies should send Theodore Roosevelt as a plenipotentiary—or "commissar" as Churchill put it—to Moscow after Vladimir Lenin, leader of the Communist revolution, had pulled Russia out of the war. In exchange for Russia re-entering the war, the Allies would "safeguard the permanent fruits of the Revolution."

"Let us never forget," Churchill argued, "that Lenin and Trotsky are fighting with ropes round their necks. They will leave office for the grave. Show them any real chance of consolidating their power … and they would be non-human not to embrace it."

WHEN ROOSEVELT MET CHURCHILL

In July 1918, Franklin D. Roosevelt met Churchill for the first time. He had been sent

Minister of Munitions Winston Churchill in Lille, northern France, 1918, watching a march past of British 47th Division troops who had liberated the town eleven days earlier.

to Britain to inspect American naval facilities. On July 29, Roosevelt attended a banquet in Gray's Inn, one of the four ancient Inns of Court in London. Churchill, then Minister of Munitions, was also there. Roosevelt was unexpectedly called on to make a speech in which he mentioned "the necessity for more of this intimate personal relationship" between the Allied nations, saying:

> It is quite impossible … to sit at home three thousand miles or more away and to obtain that close man-to-man, shoulder-to-shoulder touch, which today characterizes the work of the Allies in conducting the war.

Churchill was in the audience and recalled in his memoirs being impressed by Roosevelt's "magnificent presence in all his youth and strength," though some doubt he did actually remember the occasion. Roosevelt certainly remembered. In 1939, he told Joseph Kennedy, US Ambassador to the court of St. James's: "I have always disliked him since the time I went to England in 1918. He acted like a stinker at a dinner I attended, lording it over all of us."

The fact that Churchill clearly did not remember the occasion irritated Roosevelt even more. Roosevelt moved on to France to see the horrors of war for himself, saying later:

> I have seen war on land and sea. I have seen blood running from the wounded. I have seen men coughing out their gassed lungs. I have seen the dead in the mud. I have seen cities destroyed. I have seen two hundred limping, exhausted men come out of line—the survivors of a regiment of one thousand that went forward forty-eight hours before. I have seen children starving. I have seen the agony of mothers and wives. I hate war.

Churchill was similarly disillusioned by the slaughter of World War I, writing in 1930:

> War, which used to be cruel and magnificent, has now become cruel and squalid. Instead of a small number of well-trained professionals championing their country's cause with ancient weapons and a beautiful intricacy of archaic maneuver, sustained at every moment by the applause of their nation, we now have entire populations, including even women and children, pitted against one another in brutish mutual extermination, and only a set of bleary-eyed clerks left to add up the butcher's bill.

IN THE TWINKLING OF AN EYE

With the war over, the Liberal Party split. Lloyd George led the country as the head of a coalition of Conservatives and Coalition Liberals, with Churchill tagging along. In the new government, Churchill became Secretaries of War and Air. He now feared that the new Bolshevik state in Russia was a greater danger than the Kaiser's Germany had been and he urged the Allies to be magnanimous to the defeated nations, or as he put it to Asquith's daughter Violet: "Kill the Bolshie, kiss the Hun."

Churchill was keen to keep the fourteen-thousand British troops in Russia after the war to strangle the newborn Bolshevik state. He also wanted to support the White—anti-Communist—forces fighting the Reds in the Civil War. But after four years of war, Britain was exhausted and there was little support in the country for an Allied intervention in Russia.

Churchill became Colonial Secretary in 1921, negotiating an Anglo-Irish agreement with the new Irish Free State. Following the collapse of the Ottoman Empire, he was also responsible for British policy in the Middle East.

During the 1922 general election, he suffered from appendicitis and found himself unseated.

"In the twinkling of an eye," he said, "I found myself without an office, without a seat, without a party, and without an appendix."

WORLD IN CRISIS

Heckled at public meetings with people shouting "What about Gallipoli?" Churchill set about writing his own history of the war, *The World in Crisis*. It got some tough reviews, but Roosevelt read the book and discussed it with Felix Frankfurter, an admirer of Churchill and later a US Supreme Court judge. Frankfurter said he and Roosevelt gave Churchill something better than a suspended sentence as a writer.

The book netted Churchill £20,000 which he used to buy Chartwell, his country house in Kent. Losing again at the general election in 1923, he stood in a 1924 by-election as an "Independent Anti-Socialist" and was returned to parliament. In the general election that year, he stood successfully as a "Constitutionalist" and was appointed Chancellor of the Exchequer in the Conservative government. He put sterling on the gold standard, which led to deflation, unemployment, and the General Strike.

Out of office after the general election of 1929, he set about writing *Marlborough: His Life and Times*, a massive reassessment of his distinguished forebear, John Churchill, 1st Duke of Marlborough, who had created a Grand Alliance to defeat Louis XIV in the War of the Spanish Succession. Some see this as the inspiration for Churchill's alliance-building strategy during World War II. When the book was published in 1933, he sent a copy to Roosevelt, wishing him luck with his presidency.

THE GREATEST CRUSADE

Meanwhile, Roosevelt had been making steady headway with his political career in the interwar years. In 1920 he won the nomination for vice president on the Democratic ticket, but lost in a Republican landslide. The following year, while on vacation at Campobello Island, the family's summer retreat off the coast of Maine, he was stricken with poliomyelitis.

While he was recuperating, Eleanor kept his name alive in Democratic circles. Unable to walk, he campaigned successfully to become governor of New York in 1928 from the back of an automobile.

During a trip to the US in 1929, Churchill tried to make contact with Roosevelt, but the newly elected governor snubbed him. Returning on another lucrative lecture tour in 1931, Churchill was hit by a car in Manhattan. When he got back to England it was discovered he was still suffering from internal bleeding.

In 1932, Roosevelt won the nomination and the presidency, offering a "New Deal" for Americans suffering in the fallout from the Wall Street crash. In his inscription in the volume of *Marlborough* he sent to Roosevelt, Churchill described the New Deal as "the greatest crusade of modern times." This was mere flattery. Churchill had little time for such policies. He was much more enthusiastic that the Democrats brought an end to prohibition.

Before his inauguration Roosevelt survived an assassination attempt in Miami where the Mayor of Chicago traveling with him was mortally wounded. Unperturbed, Roosevelt ordered his car to stop, so it could take the mayor to the hospital on the backseat beside him. In his inaugural address, he told America—and the world—then in the throes of the Great Depression, that "the only thing we have to fear is fear itself."

IN THE POLITICAL WILDERNESS

While Roosevelt kept Churchill at arm's length, his son James visited him at Chartwell. Over dinner, Churchill asked his guests what was their fondest wish. When it came to his turn to answer, Churchill said without hesitation: "I wish to be prime minister and in close and daily communication by telephone with the president of the United States. There is nothing we could not do if we were together."

Churchill then asked for a piece of paper, on which he drew a pound sign and a dollar sign intertwined. Handing it to James Roosevelt, Churchill said: "Pray, bear this to your father from me. Tell him this must be the currency of the future."

"What will you call the new currency?" James Roosevelt inquired.

"The sterling dollar," Churchill replied.

"What, sir, if my father should wish to call it the dollar sterling?" the young Roosevelt asked with a grin.

Churchill beamed, saying: "We are together."

This was all wishful thinking. Churchill was in the political wilderness. In the aftermath of World War I, the world turned toward pacifism. But Churchill was out of step. In *The World Crisis* he wrote: "The story of the human race is war. Except for brief and precarious interludes there has never been peace in the world; and before history began, murderous strife was universal and unending."

THE TRUTH ABOUT HITLER

In 1928, US Secretary of State Frank B. Kellogg and French Foreign Minister Aristide Briand cooked up the Kellogg-Briand Pact, renouncing war as an instrument of national policy. It was also signed by Australia, Belgium, Canada, Czechoslovakia, Germany, British India, the Irish Free State, Italy, Japan, New Zealand, Poland, South Africa, and the United Kingdom. In all, sixty-two nations agreed to adhere to it. The US also passed a series of Neutrality Acts in 1935, 1936, 1937, and 1939.

However, in 1931 Japan invaded China. Then in 1935, Italy, under the Fascist dictator Benito Mussolini, invaded Abyssinia, now Ethiopia. Adolf Hitler had come to power in Germany in 1933 and by 1935 was openly rearming. In *The Strand Magazine* in 1935, Churchill published an article called "The Truth About Hitler," warning that Hitler had come to power by violence and was determined to avenge the German defeat in 1918. It warned of the Nazi's persecution of Jews and extra-judicial killings. He went on:

> *The United States, while preaching disarmament, continued to make enormous developments in her army, navy, and air force. France, deprived of the promised United States guarantee and confronted with the gradual revival of Germany with its tremendous military population, naturally refused to reduce her defences below the danger point. Italy, for other reasons, increased her armaments. Only England cut her defenses by land and sea far below the safety level, and appeared quite unconscious of the new peril which was developing in the air.*

WITH A HEAVY HEART

The article was reprinted in 1937 in Churchill's book *Great Contemporaries* with a portrait of Hitler alongside a portrait of Franklin Roosevelt.

"Trained in public affairs, connected with the modern history of the United States by a famous name, at forty-two he was struck down by infantile paralysis," wrote Churchill, going on to say:

> *His lower limbs refused their office. Crutches or assistance were needed for the smallest movement from place to place. To ninety-nine men out of a hundred such an affliction would have terminated all forms of public activity except those of the mind. He refused to accept this sentence. He fought against it with that same rebellion against commonly-adopted conventions which we now see in his policy.*

Already Churchill saw Roosevelt as an ally against Hitler's Germany and Stalin's Soviet Union, asking in print:

> *Will he succeed or will he fail? This is not the question we set ourselves, and to prophesy is cheap. But succeed or fail, his impulse is one which makes towards the fuller life of the masses of the people in every land, and which as it glows the brighter may well eclipse both the lurid flames of German Nordic national self-assertion and the baleful unnatural lights which are diffused from Soviet Russia.*

Although America remained staunchly isolationist, Roosevelt invited a series of dignitaries to visit him at Hyde Park.

"Convinced that bad things were going to happen in Europe," Eleanor wrote, "he wanted to make contacts with those he hoped would preserve and adhere to democracy and prove to be allies against Fascism when the conflict came."

In June 1939, it was the turn of the British King George VI and Queen Elizabeth who were visiting the US. As they left Hyde Park, Eleanor wrote: "One thought of the clouds that hung over them and the worries they were going to face and turned away and left the scene with a heavy heart."

ADOLF HITLER

Born in Austria, Adolf Hitler (1889 – 1945) was brought up in Linz. He dreamt of becoming an artist but was refused entry to the Academy of Fine Arts in Vienna and became a down-and-out. He moved to Munich in Germany. When World War I broke out in 1914, he was found unfit to join the Austrian Army. Instead, he joined the 16th Bavarian Reserve Infantry Regiment and served in the trenches on the Western Front where he enjoyed the discipline and camaraderie of combat, and won several awards for bravery. On October 15, 1918, he was temporarily blinded by mustard gas. However, he was left with a belief in the heroic virtues of war.

After the Armistice, Hitler joined the German Workers' Party, renaming it the National Socialist German Workers' Party (NSDAP or Nazi Party) and becoming its head. In the aftermath of a failed coup attempt by the Nazi Party to seize power in 1923, he published his autobiography *Mein Kampf* (My Struggle), spelling out his anti-semitic racist creed.

In 1930, the Nazis won 18 percent of the vote and 107 seats in the Reichstag, Germany's federal parliament. The following year, he became Chancellor, with 44 percent of the vote, and seized dictatorial powers over what he called the Third Reich.

In contravention of the Treaty of Versailles, Hitler began to rearm Germany and signed treaties with Fascist Italy and Imperial Japan. He annexed Austria in 1938, and seized Czechoslovakia. After signing a Non-Aggression Pact with Soviet Russia, he invaded Poland. France and Britain then declared war on Nazi Germany in 1939. The German Army quickly invaded Western Europe, but failed to take Britain. In 1941, Hitler invaded Russia and declared war on America, when Japan attacked Pearl Harbor.

Germany was defeated by the Russians in the east and by the British in North Africa. After an Anglo-American force established a firm grip in Italy, the Western Allies landed in strength in Normandy in June 1944. Germany was besieged from all sides. On April 30, 1945, with the Soviet Army fighting its way into Berlin, Hitler committed suicide by swallowing a cyanide capsule and shooting himself in the head.

CHURCHILL'S WAR OF WORDS

In reaction to Churchill's article in *The Strand Magazine*, the German government protested. *The New York Times* carried the story under the headline: "Germans Protest Churchill Attack As Libeling Hitler."

BERLIN, Oct. 30.—An official communiqué announced today that the German Ambassador to Great Britain had been ordered to protest an article by Winston Churchill in The Strand Magazine of London, on the ground that it attacks Chancellor Hitler in "malicious fashion."

"Former English Cabinet Minister Churchill had published in The Strand Magazine an article which attacks in almost unsurpassably malicious fashion National Socialism and its Fuehrer," says the communiqué. "The magazine, which has given itself to such agitations, is prohibited in the Reich for an unlimited period."

"In view of the libels against the German head of the State contained in Churchill's remarks, the German Ambassador to London has been empowered to call attention to unheard-of remarks by a member of the government party and to protest sharply to the proper authorities."

The newspaper also carried Churchill's riposte:

LONDON. Oct. 30.—Winston Churchill is apparently unrepentant despite German indignation over his magazine attack on Hitler, for in an election speech tonight he again referred to the Nazi chieftain as justification for British rearmament. "When you see the German dictator setting the whole of his people working on munitions," said Mr. Churchill, "I do not think you should allow this country to go on without doing something."

The Strand Magazine, November 1935, featuring Churchill's article "The Truth About Hitler."

PART TWO

WAR IN EUROPE

We shall fight on the beaches, we shall fight on the landing grounds, we shall fight in the fields and in the streets, we shall fight in the hills; we shall never surrender.

Winston Churchill 1940

CHAPTER 5

THE GATHERING STORM

As Churchill had warned, Hitler was recklessly intent on war. In 1936, he had sent troops into the Rhineland, a zone that had been demilitarized under the Versailles Treaty at the end of World War I. In 1938, Germany had annexed Austria. Next Hitler claimed the Sudetenland, a region of Czechoslovakia largely populated by ethnic Germans. This was conceded by British Prime Minister Neville Chamberlain in the Munich Agreement, against the wishes of the Czech government. Outside 10 Downing Street, he announced "… a British Prime Minister has returned from Germany bringing peace with honor. I believe it is peace for our time."

HITLER ADVANCES

Although Hitler promised he had no further territorial demands in Europe, Germany occupied the rest of Czechoslovakia in March 1939. In May, Hitler and Italy's leader Mussolini signed the Pact of Steel linking their two countries politically and militarily. Japan joined the alliance in September 1940, in the Tripartite Pact.

Hitler then demanded the port of Danzig—modern-day Gdansk. A Polish port, it had been seized by Prussia in 1772 and later absorbed into a united Germany. The Versailles Treaty made it a "Free City" under the League of Nations mandate, though it lay in the narrow

PEACE FOR OUR TIME

The settlement of the Czechoslovakian problem, which has now been achieved is, in my view, only the prelude to a larger settlement in which all Europe may find peace. This morning I had another talk with the German Chancellor, Herr Hitler, and here is the paper which bears his name upon it as well as mine.

British Prime Minister Neville Chamberlain landed triumphantly at Heston Aerodrome, London, on September 30, 1938, waving the Anglo-German agreement with Hitler's signature and receiving loud cheers from the crowd. The speech is now mainly remembered for its cruel irony as the signed agreement was seen to be worthless and naive less than a year later, when Hitler invaded Poland, and war was declared on September 3, 1939.

Chamberlain led Britain through the first eight months of World War II, but ill-health forced him to resign the premiership on May 10, 1940, to be replaced by Churchill. He died of cancer six months after leaving office.

Neville Chamberlain at Heston Aerodrome, 1938.

corridor that gave Poland access to the Baltic. This Polish Corridor also split East Prussia off from the rest of Germany.

The Poles refused any alteration in the status of Danzig, so the Nazis began smuggling arms and military advisors into the city. Britain and France promised to go to Poland's aid. But after the Allies abandonment of Czechoslovakia, it seemed an empty pledge. The only nation who could guarantee Poland's security was the Soviet Union, who Britain and France began to woo.

GERMAN–SOVIET PACT

On August 23, Soviet leader Joseph Stalin shocked the world by signing a Non-Aggression Pact with Germany. In a secret protocol, Germany and the Soviet Union agreed to divide Poland and the rest of Eastern Europe between them. That day Roosevelt cut short a fishing trip off Campobello and returned to Washington, while Churchill returned to England after inspecting France's defensive Maginot Line and taking a short holiday in Dreux. He had already warned America what was coming in a broadcast on NBC on August 8 called "A Hush Over Europe," saying that Britain and France were still praying for peace:

> *But in Germany, on a mountain peak, there sits one man who in a single day can release the world from the fear which now oppresses it; or in a single day can plunge all that we have and are, into a volcano of smoke and flame. If Herr Hitler does not make war, there will be no war … the whole life of mankind is dependent upon the virtues, the caprice, or the wickedness of a single man.*

WAR WITH GERMANY

On September 1, 1939, Hitler invaded western Poland. Britain had given Germany a deadline for her withdrawal from Poland—9 a.m. on September 3. Two hours after the deadline had passed, Prime Minister Neville Chamberlain declared war. At 11:30 a.m. he made a famous radio broadcast announcing:

> *This morning the British Ambassador in Berlin handed the German Government a final note stating that, unless we heard from them by eleven o'clock that they were prepared at once to withdraw their troops from Poland, a state of war would exist between us. I have to tell you now that no such undertaking has been received, and that consequently this country is at war with Germany.*

Moments later an air-raid siren went off and Churchill retreated to an air-raid shelter with a bottle of brandy. After the all-clear sounded, Chamberlain summoned Churchill to 10 Downing Street and offered him his old post of First Lord of the Admiralty and by 6 p.m. in the evening he was back at his desk there. By then, France had declared war on Germany too.

Stalin and Ribbentrop at the signing of the Non-Aggression Pact between Germany and Russia, August 1939.

BRILLIANT, ERRATIC, AND UNSAFE

Although the September 4 issue of *Time* magazine had gone to press too early to report that war had been declared, it was Churchill not Chamberlain who was on the front cover. The cover story, headlined "Vision, Vindication," said:

> *For six bitter, hog-ridden years he had pounded on his argument as tenaciously as Cato the Elder demanding the destruction of Carthage: that a rearmed and rearming Nazi Germany was a menace to Britain, to the Empire, to free speech, to Parliament. To Britons newly enraged by the German-Soviet Pact, he had been terribly justified.*

Time was unsure that Churchill would be back in the cabinet as "Britain's ruling class considers him brilliant, erratic, unsafe; certainly Prime Minister Chamberlain would regard his entry a major calamity." On the other hand: "Young Churchill was groomed to rule from the start, never let himself or his friends forget it."

Churchill was already well known in America. On top of his lecture and book tours, he had already been on the cover of *Time* twice before, once in 1923 when he published the first volume of *The World in Crisis* and again in 1925 after becoming Chancellor of the Exchequer.

THE WAR IS REALLY ON

As First Lord of the Admiralty, Churchill was indeed in the cabinet. And there was someone other than Chamberlain who considered this a calamity—Adolf Hitler. In his memoirs *Inside the Third Reich*, Albert Speer, Hitler's chief architect and later Minister for Armaments and War Production, said of Hitler:

> *He stuck unswervingly to his opinion that the West was too feeble, too worn out, and too decadent to begin the war seriously. Probably it was also embarrassing for him to admit to his entourage and above all to himself that he had made so crucial a mistake. I still remember his consternation when the news*

Air Commodore Winston Churchill buckles up before a flight, 1939.

came that Churchill was going to enter the British War Cabinet as First Lord of the Admiralty. With this ill-omened press report in his hand, Goering stepped out of the door of Hitler's salon. He dropped into the nearest chair and said wearily: "Churchill in the Cabinet. That means that the war is really on. Now we shall have war with England." From these and other observations I deduced that this initiation of real war was not what Hitler had projected.

THE GIGANTIC CONFLICT

The news was not well received in Washington either. When Ambassador Kennedy visited the White House that summer, he told Roosevelt, who already thought Churchill was a "stinker": "He had developed into a fine two-handed drinker and his judgment never proved good."

Kennedy's impression was that Churchill was "always sucking on a whisky bottle." Under Secretary of State Sumner Welles also referred to Churchill as "a drunken sot" and a "third- or fourth-rate man."

Kennedy also warned that Churchill sought to lure the United States into the war solely to preserve the British Empire. "I'm willing to help them all I can but don't want them to play me for a sucker," Roosevelt told Kennedy.

However Roosevelt knew he had little choice. In his radio "fireside chat" of September 3, 1939, he said:

Tonight my single duty is to speak to the whole of America. Until 4:30 this morning I had hoped against hope that some miracle would prevent a devastating war in Europe and bring to an end the invasion of Poland by Germany. For four long years a succession of actual wars and constant crises have shaken the entire world and have threatened in each case to bring on the gigantic conflict which is today unhappily a fact ... When the peace has been broken anywhere, peace of all countries everywhere is in danger. It is easy for you and for me to shrug our shoulders and say that conflicts taking place thousands of miles from the continental United States, and,

indeed thousands of miles from the whole American hemisphere, do not seriously affect the Americas—and that all the United States has to do is to ignore them and go about its own business. Passionately though we may desire detachment, we are forced to realize that every word that comes through the air, every ship that sails the sea, every battle that is fought, does affect the American future.

KEEPING AMERICAN WATERS SAFE

As there was no possibility of the United States joining the war at that point, Roosevelt thought that Britain, possibly under Churchill, might provide a bulwark against the onslaught of Hitler, who seemed obsessed with world domination. On September 11, he wrote Churchill a letter:

My dear Churchill:—

It is because you and I occupied similar positions in the World War that I want you to know how glad I am that you are back again in the Admiralty. Your problems are, I realize, complicated by new factors but the essential is not very different. What I want you and the Prime Minister to know is that I shall at all times welcome it if you will keep me in touch personally with anything you want me to know about. You can always send sealed letters through your pouch or my pouch.

I am glad you did the Marlboro volumes before this thing started—and I much enjoyed reading them.

With my sincere regards,
Faithfully yours,
Franklin D. Roosevelt

Churchill replied by telegram, headed "The following from Naval person" and saying: "Your letter takes me back to 1914 and it is certainly a most unusual experience to occupy the same post fighting the same enemy 25 years later."

However, that sentence was deleted from the official reply which proposed a three-hundred-mile safety belt around the Americas where no submarines of any belligerent nation should act. But if German raiders operated from or took refuge in the American zone, the British demanded the right to be protected or protect themselves.

Churchill's first wartime telegram to Roosevelt ended: "We wish to help you in every way in keeping war out of American waters."

THE PHONE CALL

That night Churchill was having dinner in his London apartment with Rear-Admiral Bruce Fraser when the phone rang. According to Fraser, Churchill, "who rather disliked telephones," asked the butler: "Who is it?"

The butler said: "I don't know, sir."

"Well, say I can't attend to it right now," snapped Churchill.

"I think you ought to come, sir," said the butler.

Fraser said that Churchill "got up rather testily. Then we heard his replies, 'Yes, sir … No, sir.'"

"Do you know who that was?" asked Churchill after he had put the phone down. "The President of the United States. It is remarkable to think of being rung up in this little flat in Victoria Street by the President himself in the midst of a great war. This is very important and I must go and see the Prime Minister at once."

Roosevelt had said that a warning had just been given on German radio that the US steamship *Iroquois* was going to be sunk, implying that this was the work of the Royal Navy—or indeed, Churchill himself. Churchill knew the dangers. German propaganda had tried to blame him for the sinking of the *Lusitania* in 1915. As it was, the *Iroquois* arrived back in port in New York unmolested.

OUR AMERICAN FRIEND

When a German submarine sank the *Royal Oak* on October 14, Churchill prepared an account of the action for Roosevelt, knowing his interest in naval matters. He was eager to develop the relationship.

German troops advancing during the invasion of Denmark and Norway, 1940.

"I think we ought to send something more to our American friend in order to keep him interested in our affairs," Churchill told the First Sea Lord, Admiral Sir Dudley Pound. "If you think of anything else which could be added with advantage, please pencil it in. We must not let the liaison lapse."

A few days later, Churchill offered Roosevelt details of Britain's ASDIC anti-submarine location device. Roosevelt was keen, but the British Air Ministry asked for the specifications of the Norden bombsight in exchange and, for the moment, the deal foundered.

At the end of October, British press baron Lord Beaverbrook wrote to Roosevelt, saying: "If Chamberlain falls, Churchill will succeed him, forming a coalition government."

When Joseph Kennedy visited the White House again in December, Roosevelt said he was keeping in with Churchill because "there is a strong possibility that he will become prime minister, and I want to get my hand in now."

WALKING WITH DESTINY

German forces marched into Denmark and Norway on April 6, 1940. In return Churchill sent an expeditionary force, but the landings at Trondheim were quickly overwhelmed and the troops had to be evacuated. Critics called it a second Gallipoli. But when the matter was debated in parliament, Churchill put up a spirited defense. After a narrow vote, Chamberlain realized that there would have to be a coalition government and, as Labour would refuse to serve under him, he would have to resign.

At a meeting to discuss the succession, Churchill held his tongue. The only other candidate, the Foreign Secretary Lord Halifax, spoke up, saying that he did not think it was appropriate that a member of the House of Lords should be prime minister, so Churchill got the job. At 6 p.m. on May 10, he accepted the King's invitation to form a government.

"I felt," he wrote, "as though I were walking with destiny and that all my past life had been a preparation for this hour and for this trial."

A SWIFTLY DARKENING SCENE

Churchill's appointment was discussed in the White House the following day. Roosevelt's Interior Secretary Harold Ickes said: "Apparently Churchill is very unreliable when under the influence of drink." At age 65, he was also considered too old.

Assistant Secretary of State Adolf Berle also said he was too old and tired, while Sumner Welles, who had visited Churchill in March, said he was unsteady and drank too much. Roosevelt had his doubts too but, writing in his diary, Ickes noted: "The President said that he supposed that Churchill was the best man that England had, even if he was drunk half of his time." Eleanor Roosevelt dismissed Churchill as "reactionary." Meanwhile in a speech in the House of Commons, Churchill offered the British people nothing "but blood, toil, tears, and sweat."

With German armies pouring into the Low Countries and threatening France, Churchill cabled Roosevelt:

Most Secret and Personal. President Roosevelt from Former Naval Person.

Although I have changed my office, I am sure you would not wish me to discontinue our intimate, private correspondence. As you are no doubt aware, the scene has darkened swiftly. The enemy have a marked preponderance in the air, and their new technique is making a deep impression upon the French. I think myself the battle on land has only just begun, and I should like to see tanks engaged. Up to the present, Hitler is working with specialized units in tanks and air. The small countries are simply smashed up, one by one, like matchwood. We must expect, though it is not yet certain, that Mussolini will hurry in to share the loot of civilization. We expect to be attacked here ourselves, both from the air and by parachute and airborne troops in the near future, and are getting ready for them. If necessary, we shall continue the war alone and we are not afraid of that. But I trust you realize, Mr. President, that the voice and force of the United States may count for nothing if they are withheld too long. You may have a completely subjugated, Nazified Europe established with astonishing swiftness, and the weight may be more than we can bear. All I ask now is that you should proclaim nonbelligerency, which would mean that you would help us with everything short of actually engaging armed forces.

STRAINED TO BREAKING POINT

Then Churchill asked for the loan of forty or fifty of America's older destroyers to bridge the gap between what the British already had and the large number whose construction had been put in hand at the beginning of the war. "This time next year we shall have plenty," he said. "But if in the interval Italy comes in against us with another one hundred submarines, we may be strained to breaking point."

He also wanted several hundred of the latest types of aircraft which the US army were then taking delivery of. These could be exchanged for those now being constructed for the British in the United States. Then there was anti-aircraft equipment and ammunition, "of which again there will be plenty next year, if we are alive to see it."

British supplies of iron ore from Sweden, North Africa, and northern Spain were under threat, so it was also necessary to purchase steel in the United States, along with other materials.

"We shall go on paying dollars for as long as we can," he said, "but I should like to feel reasonably sure that when we can pay no more, you will give us the stuff all the same."

He then told Roosevelt that he had many reports of possible German parachute or airborne descents in Ireland, and asked whether a United States squadron could visit Irish ports, possibly for a prolonged stay.

Finally, he said: "I am looking to you to keep that Japanese dog quiet in the Pacific, using Singapore in any way convenient. The details of the material which we have in mind will be communicated to you separately." And he signed off: "With all good wishes and respect."

FIGHTING ON FOREVER

Although Roosevelt had his doubts about Churchill's chances against Hitler, there was no doubt that he would fight on forever. If German forces occupied Britain, Churchill told Kennedy that he would move the government to Canada and fight on from there. Lord Lothian, the British Ambassador to Washington, also assured Roosevelt that, if necessary, Churchill would send the Royal Navy to the US or Canada to keep it out of German hands.

The following day Roosevelt replied via the US Embassy, saying: "Please transmit the following from the President to the former naval person." The body of the cable read:

I have just received your message and I am sure it is unnecessary for me to say that I am most happy to continue our private correspondence as we have in the past.

I am, of course, giving every possible consideration to the suggestions made in your message. I shall take up your specific proposals one by one.

First, with regard to the possible loan of forty or fifty of our older destroyers. As you know a step of that kind could not be taken except with the specific authorization of the Congress and I am not certain that it would be wise for that suggestion to be made to the Congress at this moment. Furthermore, it seems to me doubtful, from the standpoint of our own defense requirements, which must inevitably be linked with the defense requirements of this hemisphere and with our obligations in the Pacific, whether we could dispose even temporarily of these destroyers. Furthermore, even if we were able to take the step you suggest, it would be at least six or seven weeks at a minimum, as I see it, before these vessels could undertake active service under the British flag.

Second. We are now doing everything within our power to make it possible for the Allied Governments to obtain the latest types of aircraft in the United States.

Third. If Mr. Purvis may receive immediate instructions to discuss the question of anti-aircraft equipment and ammunition with the appropriate authorities here in Washington, the most favorable consideration will be given to the request made in the light of our own defense needs and requirements.

Fourth. Mr. Purvis has already taken up with the appropriate authorities here the purchase of steel in the United States and I understand that satisfactory arrangements have been made.

Fifth. I shall give further consideration to your suggestion with regard to the visit of the United States Squadron to Irish ports.

Sixth. As you know, the American fleet is now concentrated at Hawaii where it will remain at least for the time being.

I shall communicate with you again as soon as I feel able.

The best of luck to you.
Franklin Roosevelt.

[Arthur Purvis, a Canadian, was head of the British Purchasing Commission which coordinated the purchase of war materials in the US.]

CONQUER WE SHALL

By then France was being overrun, so on May 18, 1940, Churchill wrote:

I do not need to tell you about the gravity of what has happened. We are determined to persevere to the very end whatever the result of the great battle raging in France may be. We must expect in any case to be attacked here on the Dutch model before very long and we hope to give a good account of ourselves. But if American assistance is to play any part it must be available soon.

But Roosevelt was doing all he could. While 95 percent of Americans wanted to stay out of the war, 62 percent agreed that the US should do everything possible to help Britain and France, short of going to war. So in November 1939,

Roosevelt allowed arms sales to belligerent nations—that is, Britain and France—on a cash-and-carry basis.

Meanwhile Churchill turned to the radio again, knowing that Roosevelt would be listening. In a blunt but inspiring broadcast on May 19, he said:

Our task is not only to win the battle—but to win the war. After this battle in France abates its force, there will come the battle for our Island—for all that Britain is, and all that Britain means. That will be the struggle. In that supreme emergency we shall not hesitate to take every step, even the most drastic, to call forth from our people the last ounce and the last inch of effort of which they are capable. The interests of property, the hours of labor, are nothing compared with the struggle of life and honor, for right and freedom, to which we have vowed ourselves … now one bond unites us all—to wage war until victory is won, and never to surrender ourselves to servitude and shame, whatever the cost and the agony may be. This is one of the most awe-striking periods in the long history of France and Britain. It is also beyond doubt the most sublime. Side by side, unaided except by their kith and kin in the great Dominions and by the wide empires which rest beneath their shield—side by side, the British and French peoples have advanced to rescue not only Europe but mankind from the foulest and most soul-destroying tyranny which has ever darkened and stained the pages of history. Behind them—behind us—behind the Armies and Fleets of Britain and France—gather a group of shattered States and bludgeoned races: the Czechs, the Poles, the Norwegians, the Danes, the Dutch, the Belgians—upon all of whom the long night of barbarism will descend, unbroken even by a star of hope, unless we conquer, as conquer we must; as conquer we shall.

CHAPTER 6

WE SHALL NEVER SURRENDER

What Roosevelt's reaction was to Churchill's broadcast of May 19, 1940, is not recorded. But Eleanor was impressed. Churchill's speeches, she said, "were a tonic to us here in the United States as to his own people … In some ways he was more blunt with the people of Great Britain than my husband ever was with us." And she admired him for it.

On May 20, Churchill wrote to Roosevelt again:

Secret and Personal for the President from Former Naval Person

Lothian has reported his conversation with you. I understand your difficulties, but I am very sorry about the destroyers. If they were here in six weeks they would play an invaluable part. The battle in France is full of danger to both sides. Though we have taken heavy toll of the enemy in the air and are clawing down two or three to one of their planes, they have still a formidable numerical superiority. Our most vital need is, therefore, the delivery at the earliest possible date of the largest possible number of Curtiss P–40 fighters, now in course of delivery to your Army.

With regard to the closing part of your talk with Lothian, our intention is, whatever happens, to fight on to the end in this island, and, provided we can get the help for which we ask, we hope to run them very close in the air battles in view of individual superiority. Members of the present administration would likely go down during this process should it result adversely, but in no conceivable circumstances will we consent to surrender. If members of the present administration were finished and others came in to parley amid the ruins, you must not be blind to

the fact that the sole remaining bargaining counter with Germany would be the Fleet, and if this country was left by the United States to its fate no one would have the right to blame those then responsible if they made the best terms they could for the surviving inhabitants. Excuse me, Mr. President, putting this nightmare bluntly. Evidently I could not answer for my successors, who in utter despair and helplessness might well have to accommodate themselves to the German will. However, there is happily no need at present to dwell upon such ideas. Once more thanking you for your goodwill …

Despite the emollient closing sentence, Churchill said to Jock Colville: "Here's a telegram for those bloody Yankees. Send it off tonight."

WE SHALL FIGHT ON THE BEACHES

As the situation in France collapsed, the British Expeditionary Force sent to support the French Army withdrew to Dunkirk. From there 340,000 men were evacuated by June 4, but almost all their equipment was abandoned. Churchill's response was to make another rousing speech in the House of Commons that ended with a direct appeal to Roosevelt, an appeal that has gone down in history as one of Churchill's most famous speeches:

Even though large tracts of Europe and many old and famous States have fallen or may fall into the grip of the Gestapo and all the odious apparatus of Nazi rule, we shall not flag or fail. We shall go on to the end, we shall fight in France, we shall fight on the seas and oceans, we shall fight with growing

WINSTON CHURCHILL

Sir Winston Leonard Spencer-Churchill (1874 – 1965) was a British politician, army officer, and writer, who was Prime Minister of the United Kingdom from 1940 to 1945 and again from 1951 to 1955.

confidence and growing strength in the air, we shall defend our Island, whatever the cost may be, we shall fight on the beaches, we shall fight on the landing grounds, we shall fight in the fields and in the streets, we shall fight in the hills; we shall never surrender, and even if, which I do not for a moment believe, this Island or a large part of it were subjugated and starving, then our Empire beyond the seas, armed and guarded by the British Fleet, would carry on the struggle, until, in God's good time, the New World, with all its power and might, steps forth to the rescue and the liberation of the old.

THE HAND THAT HELD THE DAGGER

On June 10, Italy declared war on Britain and France. By coincidence, Roosevelt was scheduled to deliver the commencement address at the University of Virginia, where his son Franklin Jr. was graduating. Roosevelt seized the opportunity to address the situation in Europe:

Let us not hesitate—all of us—to proclaim certain truths. Overwhelmingly we, as a nation—and this applies to all the other American nations—are convinced that military and naval victory for the gods of force and hate would endanger the institutions of democracy in the western world, and that equally, therefore, the whole of our sympathies lies with those nations that are giving their life blood in combat against these forces. The people and the Government of the United States have seen with the utmost regret and with grave disquiet the decision of the Italian Government to engage in the hostilities now raging in Europe …

On this tenth day of June, 1940, the hand that held the dagger has struck it into the back of its neighbor. On this tenth day of June, 1940, in this University founded by the first great American teacher of democracy, we send forth our prayers and our hopes to those beyond the seas who are maintaining with magnificent valor their battle for freedom.

In our American unity, we will pursue two obvious and simultaneous courses; we will extend to the opponents of force the material resources of this nation; and, at the same time, we will harness and speed up the use of those resources in order that we ourselves in the Americas may have equipment and training equal to the task of any emergency and every defense. All roads leading to the accomplishment of these objectives must be kept clear of obstructions. We will not slow down or detour. Signs and signals call for speed—full speed ahead.

Churchill listened to this speech on the radio. It seemed that his prayers had been answered. The following day, he cabled:

We all listened to you last night and were fortified by the grand scope of your declaration. Your statement that material aid of the United States will be given to the Allies in their struggle is a strong encouragement in a dark but not unhopeful hour. Everything must be done to keep France in the fight and to prevent any idea of the fall of Paris, should it occur, becoming the occasion of any kind of parley. The hope with which you inspired them may give them strength to persevere.

He continued with a shopping list—airplanes, flying boats, and thirty or forty old destroyers to counter the number of Italian submarines that might come out into the Atlantic.

We can fit them very rapidly with our ASDICs and they will bridge over the gap of 6 months before our wartime new construction comes into play. We will return them or their equivalents to you without fail at 6 months notice if at any time you need them. The next 6 months are vital … Not a day should be lost. I send you my heartfelt thanks and those of my colleagues for all you are doing and seeking to do for what we may now indeed call a common cause.

BENITO MUSSOLINI

Mussolini (1883 – 1945) claimed to have been the son of a blacksmith—making him a "man of the people." However, his father was also a part-time socialist journalist, and so he followed his father into the field, founding his own newspaper *La Lotta di Classe* (The Class Struggle) and editing *Avanti!* (Forward!), the official socialist newspaper.

At first, he opposed Italy's involvement in World War I, then changed his mind and went to fight in the war. He was wounded, but returned home convinced that he was a man of destiny. Advocating dictatorship, he organized discontented radicals and discharged soldiers into *fasci di combattimento*—fighting bands. His Fascist party took their name from the fasces of the lictors—the symbols of ancient Roman authority.

Although Italy was on the winning side in World War I, the war left the country in a state of social and economic turmoil. This was exploited by Mussolini and his Fascist Blackshirts. On October 30, 1922, the Blackshirts marched on Rome in a show of strength, forcing the Italian King Victor Emmanuel III to invite Mussolini to form a government. This was an inspiration for Hitler and the Nazis in Germany.

When Hitler came to power, he proclaimed the Rome-Berlin axis with Mussolini. In 1939, this became the "Pact of Steel." Once France was on the verge of collapse, Mussolini declared war.

Italian forces in North Africa were then routed by the British. After an Anglo-American invasion force landed in Sicily in July 1943, Mussolini was deposed and imprisoned. That September, Mussolini was rescued by the SS. By then the Allies had established a presence in southern Italy. Mussolini was installed in a puppet state in northern Italy. When it collapsed, Mussolini was captured and shot by partisans as he was fleeing toward Switzerland. His dead body, and that of his mistress Clara Petacci, were displayed hung upside down from a lamppost in Milan.

THE MASTERY OF THE WORLD

Before Roosevelt had a chance to reply, he got another cable from Churchill, saying that he had been out to the French headquarters to see General Maxime Weygand.

> Of course I made it clear to the French that we should continue whatever happened, and that we thought Hitler could not win the war or the mastery of the world until he has disposed of us, which has not been found easy in the past, and which perhaps will not be found easy now. I made it clear to the French that we had good hopes of victory, and anyhow had no doubts whatever of what our duty was. If there is anything you can say publicly or privately to the French, now is the time.

At Churchill's behest, Roosevelt wrote to the Prime Minister of France, Paul Reynaud, forwarding the text to Churchill. It said:

> As I have already stated to you and to Mr. Churchill, this Government is doing everything in its power to make available to the Allied Governments the material they so urgently require, and our efforts to do still more are being redoubled. This is so because of our faith in and our support for the ideals for which the Allies are fighting. The magnificent resistance of the French and British armies has profoundly impressed the American people.

On June 13, Churchill told Roosevelt:

> Reynaud felt strongly that it would be beyond his power to encourage his people to fight on without hope of ultimate victory, and that hope can only be kindled by American intervention up to the extreme limit open to you. As he put it, they wanted to see light at the end of the tunnel.

There was only one thing to do—publicize the text of his telegram to Reynaud.

"Mr. President I must tell you that it seems to me absolutely vital that this message should be published tomorrow June 14 in order that it may play the decisive part in turning the course of world history. It will I am sure decide the French to deny Hitler a patched-up peace with France."

Roosevelt refused to publish it on the grounds that it might be misread. It could be taken to mean that the US was offering military support, something he had no authority to do under the Constitution. Only Congress could do that.

THE FATE OF THE FRENCH FLEET

Both being naval men, it was the fate of the French Fleet that concerned them. While understanding Roosevelt's difficulties with public opinion and Congress, Churchill asked him:

> Have you considered what offers Hitler may choose to make to France? He may say, "surrender the Fleet intact and I will leave you Alsace-Lorraine," or alternatively, "if you do not give me your ships I will destroy your towns." I am personally convinced that America will in the end go to all lengths, but this moment is supremely critical for France. A declaration that the United States will if necessary enter the war might save France. Failing that, in a few days French resistance may have crumbled and we shall be left alone.

Again Churchill assured Roosevelt that he would not hesitate to send the Royal Navy across the Atlantic if Britain was defeated, but he might not be in charge then and Britain may be no more than a vassal state in Hitler's empire:

> A pro-German Government would certainly be called into being to make peace and might present to a shattered or a starving nation an almost irresistible case for entire submission to the Nazi will. The fate of the British Fleet, as I have already mentioned to you, would be decisive on the future of the United States, because if it were joined to the Fleets of Japan, France and Italy and the great resources of German industry, overwhelming sea-power would be in Hitler's hands … This revolution in seapower might happen very quickly and certainly long before the United States would be able to prepare against it. If we go down

you may have a United States of Europe under the Nazi command far more numerous, far stronger, far better armed than the New World.

Later that evening, Churchill wrote again, saying he had heard from Reynaud and the British ambassador in Bordeaux, who said that if the United States did not come into the war at a very early day "the French will very quickly ask for an armistice." In that case, the French Fleet would fall into German hands.

"When I speak of the United States entering the war I am, of course, not thinking in terms of an expeditionary force, which I know is out of the question," said Churchill. "What I have in mind is the tremendous moral effect that such an American decision would produce, not merely in France but also in all the democratic countries of the world, and, in the opposite sense, on the German and Italian peoples."

THEIR FINEST HOUR

Churchill returned to the House of Commons on June 18, 1940, with more rousing oratory and more dire warnings for the US and Roosevelt:

What General Weygand called the Battle of France is over. I expect that the Battle of Britain is about to begin. Upon this battle depends the survival of Christian civilization. Upon it depends our own British life, and the long continuity of our institutions and our Empire. The whole fury and might of the enemy must very soon be turned on us. Hitler knows that he will have to break us in this Island or lose the war. If we can stand up to him, all Europe may be free and the life of the world may move forward into broad, sunlit uplands. But if we fail, then the whole world, including the United States, including all that we have known and cared for, will sink into the abyss of a new Dark Age made more sinister, and perhaps more protracted, by the lights of perverted science. Let us therefore brace ourselves to our duties, and so bear ourselves that, if the British Empire and its Commonwealth last for a thousand years, men will still say, "This was their finest hour."

Reynaud's government had collapsed on June 16, and the elderly Marshal Philippe Pétain, France's most honored soldier in World War I, took over. On June 22, he signed the surrender agreement and set up a puppet government in south France which was not yet occupied by the Germans. After that, the flurry of cables from Churchill to Roosevelt ceased.

For all his eloquence, Roosevelt could not decide whether Churchill was an empty blowhard. Meanwhile the US military were advising him that they had given so generously to the Allied powers that they had seriously weakened their own strength. If they gave more aid to Britain and she was defeated they would not be able to justify to the American people the risk they had taken with their own defense.

CONVINCING ROOSEVELT

Churchill was still concerned about the fate of the French Fleet which had taken refuge in the port of Mers el-Kebir in French Algeria. When the French authorities there failed to hand it over, the Royal Navy attacked it on July 3, sinking or damaging most of the ships there to prevent them falling into German hands—1,297 French sailors were killed in the action and 350 wounded. This convinced Roosevelt that Churchill was serious, and really might hold out.

Roosevelt sent William Donovan over to assess whether Britain could survive. The US ambassador Joseph Kennedy was furious as he had been reporting that the British were finished and America should have nothing more to do with them. However, Donovan was received by George VI at Buckingham Palace and Churchill in the Cabinet War Room under Whitehall. He was briefed on the operations of MI6 and the Special Operations Executive (SOE), which carried out sabotage operations in occupied Europe.

Donovan was also given unprecedented access to other intelligence facilities, though Churchill decided to hold back the intelligence coming from Bletchley Park where code-breakers were deciphering the German radio messages using the "Enigma" machines. This was vital. Churchill did not want Roosevelt to know that by October the Enigma decrypts suggested Germany's planned invasion had been postponed and, in January 1941, that Hitler had other plans. He feared that Roosevelt would not give him the backing needed if he knew that an invasion was not imminent. Both Churchill and Roosevelt loved secret intelligence and shared more as the war went on.

IN TIMES LIKE THESE

First elected in 1932, Roosevelt was due to retire in January 1941. He had already built a retirement hideaway called Top Cottage at Hyde Park and signed a deal with *Collier's* to write articles for the magazine at $75,000 a year. However, there had been speculation throughout the spring and summer of 1940 that he might run for an unprecedented third term. By convention presidents only served two terms and George Washington had refused to run a third time. (The Twenty-second Amendment to the Constitution, ratified in 1951, now prevents anyone from being elected president more than twice.)

As Nazi Germany swept through Western Europe, Roosevelt decided that only he had the necessary experience and skills to see the nation safely through the Nazi threat. He also persuaded party bosses that no other Democrat could defeat the popular Republican candidate Wendell Willkie.

Accepting the Democratic nomination at the convention in Chicago in July, Roosevelt explained why he was running again:

In times like these—in times of great tension, of great crisis —the compass of the world narrows to a single fact. The fact which dominates our world is the fact of armed aggression, the fact of successful armed aggression, aimed at the form of Government, the kind of society that we in the United States have chosen and established for ourselves. It is a fact which no one longer doubts—which no one is longer able to ignore.

It is not an ordinary war. It is a revolution imposed by force of arms, which threatens all men everywhere. It is a revolution which proposes not to set men free but to reduce them to slavery—to reduce them to slavery in the interest of a dictatorship which has already shown the nature and the extent of the advantage which it hopes to obtain.

That is the fact which dominates our world and which dominates the lives of all of us, each and every one of us. In the face of the danger which confronts our time, no individual retains or can hope to retain, the right of personal choice which free men enjoy in times of peace. He has a first obligation to serve in the defense of our institutions of freedom—a first obligation to serve his country in whatever capacity his country finds him useful.

Like most men of my age, I had made plans for myself, plans for a private life of my own choice and for my own satisfaction, a life of that kind to begin in January, 1941. These plans, like so many other plans, had been made in a world which now seems as distant as another planet. Today all private plans, all private lives, have been in a sense repealed by an overriding public danger. In the face of that public danger all those who can be of service to the Republic have no choice but to offer themselves for service in those capacities for which they may be fitted.

Those, my friends, are the reasons why I have had to admit to myself, and now to state to you, that my conscience will not let me turn my back upon a call to service.

Apart from a telegram sent via the British Embassy telling Roosevelt that the Duke of Windsor was to be made Governor of the Bahamas, there was no communication between the two leaders for eight weeks. Churchill had other things on his mind.

Presidential campaign poster from 1940, supporting the re-election of President Roosevelt.

FRANKLIN D. ROOSEVELT

Franklin Delano Roosevelt (1882 – 1945), often referred to by his initials FDR, was the 32nd President of the United States from 1933 until his death in 1945. He is rated by scholars as one of the three greatest US Presidents along with George Washington and Abraham Lincoln.

CHAPTER 7

THE VOICE OF FREEDOM

During June and July 1940, France was overrun and the campaign in North Africa began with the British crossing the border from Egypt into Italian-occupied Libya. The British also disabled the French Fleet at anchor in Tunis. Britain rejected a peace offer by Hitler and the Battle of Britain began. Then on July 30, Churchill at last wrote to Roosevelt:

It is some time since I ventured to cable personally to you, and many things both good and bad have happened in between. It has now become most urgent for you to give us the destroyers, motorboats and flying-boats for which we have asked. The Germans have the whole French coastline from which to launch U-boats and dive-bomber attacks upon our trade and food, and in addition we must be constantly prepared to repel by sea action threatened invasion in the narrow waters …

Again, he stressed naval matters, knowing Roosevelt's interest:

Latterly the Air attack on our shipping has become injurious. In the last ten days we have had the following destroyers sunk: Brazen, Codrington, Delight, Wren, and the following damaged: Beagle, Boreas, Brilliant, Griffin,

Montrose, Walpole, Whitshed, total eleven. All this in the advent of any attempt which may be made at invasion. Destroyers are frightfully vulnerable to Air bombing, and yet they must be held in the Air bombing area to prevent sea-borne invasion. We could not keep up the present rate of casualties for long, and if we cannot get a substantial reinforcement, the whole fate of the war may be decided by this minor and easily remediable factor. I cannot understand why, with the position as it is, you do not send me at least 50 or 60 of your oldest destroyers …

Mr. President, with great respect, I must tell you that in the long history of the world, this is a thing to do now.

THE LEND-LEASE

Roosevelt at last relented—in exchange for ninety-nine-year leases on bases in Newfoundland, Bermuda, the Bahamas, and the British West Indies. The purpose of this, he explained in a cable, that such assistance could "only be furnished if the American people and the Congress frankly recognized that in return

To prevent the ships falling into enemy hands, the British destroyed the French Fleet at Mers el-Kebir on the coast of French Algeria on July 3, 1940.

therefore the national defense and security of the United States would be enhanced." In fact, with the election approaching, Roosevelt did not dare to take this to Congress and gave the British the ships by executive order.

Churchill accepted the ships-for-bases deal on August 15, saying:

> *The moral value of this fresh aid from your government and people at this critical time will be very great and widely felt …*
>
> *We intend to fight this out here to the end, and none of us would ever buy peace by surrendering or scuttling the fleet … The spirit of our people is splendid. Their confidence in the issue has been enormously and legitimately strengthened by the severe air fighting of the passed weeks …*
>
> *Once again, Mr. President, let me thank you for your help and encouragement which means so much to us.*

THE FEW

Later Roosevelt recalled a conversation he had with Churchill over the matter: "Winston said: 'Now how in the heck am I going to explain this to the British people? They will say the Americans are taking our territory.' I said, 'Listen, Winston, those places are nothing but a headache to you—you know that.'"

Roosevelt also said that he had told Churchill the British possessions in the Caribbean and the Atlantic were too costly and a headache for another reason: "Furthermore, these places are inhabited by some eight million dark-skinned gentlemen and I don't want them coming to this country and adding to the problem which we already have with our thirteen million black men. I tell you, Winston, it is just a headache and you can keep it."

The Battle of Britain was beginning. After visiting the operations room of No. 11 Group, Fighter Command, and seeing that every single squadron was engaged with the enemy, Churchill came up with the line: "Never in the field of human conflict has so much been owed by so many to so few."

STEADFAST ENGLISH EYES

On August 1, Hitler had ordered his air force to attack the British Royal Air Force's bases in preparation for a seaborne invasion across the English Channel. Late in the evening of August 24, a German plane accidentally dropped bombs on non-military targets in London. Churchill immediately ordered a retaliatory attack on Berlin.

The next night, eighty-one bombers took off for the German capital. Only twenty-nine planes made it back. The damage to Berlin was slight but it infuriated Hitler who switched the attack from the RAF's airfields to the terror bombing of London and other British cities, known as the Blitz. But with the RAF still dominating the skies over Britain, Hitler had to postpone, and then cancel his invasion.

Eight months of constant bombing did not quell the spirit of the British. American heiress cum British member of parliament Nancy Astor said: "To see them, gazing at their home, now a heap of ashes, their neighbors dead, and sometimes their own families too, and yet they look at you with steadfast English eyes and say, 'Hitler won't beat us this way.'"

The British scientist and writer C.P. Snow remarked: "We were sustained by a surge of national emotion, of which Churchill was both symbol and essence, evocator and voice."

He certainly remained that symbol in America. On September 30, 1940, Churchill was on the cover of *Time* magazine again. The cover story, headlined "Battle of Britain: Death and the hazards," began:

> **REWARD–DEAD OR ALIVE:**
>
> Englishman, 25 years old, about 5 ft. 8 in. tall, indifferent build, walks "with a forward stoop, pale appearance, red-brownish hair, small and hardly noticeable mustache, talks through his nose and cannot pronounce the letter S properly.
>
> On the walls and poles of the Transvaal this handbill was pasted one day during the Boer War. It described a young newspaper reporter who had fought like

"NEVER WAS SO MUCH OWED BY SO MANY TO SO FEW"

THE PRIME MINISTER

Battle of Britain propaganda poster—"Never was so much owed by so many to so few"—derived from the specific line in Churchill's famous wartime speech, referring to the valiant efforts of the RAF air crews during the Battle of Britain. Pilots who fought in the battle have been known as The Few ever since.

a professional soldier when a British armored train was ambushed by Boers; had been captured and held as prisoner of war, had climbed over the ten-foot iron fence of his prison with no map or compass, but with a little money and some cubes of chocolate in his pockets, and was eventually taken. It described and—with the exception of the age and the mustache, which was just a medal of a not-quite-certain manhood—and still does describe Winston Churchill.

This is Churchill as Hollywood action hero. The article continued: "It symbolizes Winston Churchill so aptly and lovingly symbolizes Great Britain's unwillingness to give up when apparently cornered."

On January 6, 1941, he was on the cover of *Time* yet again, this time as Man of the Year.

Naturally the American election campaign of 1940 revolved around the war. On the stump Wendell Willkie promised: "If you elect me president of the United States, no American boy will ever be sent to the shambles of a European war."

THE LIGHTS BY WHICH WE STEER

On October 30, 1940, Roosevelt matched him, telling American voters: "Your boys are not going to be sent into any foreign war." Previously, he had added the caveat "except in case of attack." Roosevelt now dropped the rider, arguing that if the US was attacked, it wasn't a foreign war.

Churchill was worried. He wrote later: "No newcomer to power could possess or soon acquire the knowledge and experience of Franklin Roosevelt. None could equal his commanding gifts." Willkie, in comparison, had little confidence in Churchill.

President Franklin Roosevelt's touring car rolls through Kingston on his way home to Hyde Park for Election Day.

Roosevelt won the election with 27.3 million votes against 22.3 million, with a majority in the Electoral College of 449 to 82.

The day after the election Churchill wrote to Roosevelt, saying:

I did not think it right for me as a Foreigner to express my opinion upon American politics while the Election was on, but now I feel you will not mind my saying that I prayed for your success and that I am truly thankful for it. This does not mean that I seek or wish for anything more than the full, fair and free play of your mind upon the world issues now at stake in which our two nations have to discharge their respective duties. We are entering upon a sombre phase of what must evidently be a protracted and broadening war, and I look forward to being able to interchange my thoughts with you in all that confidence and goodwill which has grown up between us since I went to the Admiralty at the outbreak. Things are afoot which will be remembered as long as the English language is spoken in any quarter of the globe, and in expressing the comfort I feel that the people of the United States have once again cast these great burdens upon you, I must avow my sure faith that the lights by which we steer will bring us all safely to anchor.

Roosevelt sent no reply. In another telegram ten days later, Churchill said: "I hope you got my personal telegram of congratulation." Again Roosevelt did not reply.

Between November 12 and December 7, Churchill went through several drafts of a long letter, summing up the situation as the end of the year approached and outlining the prospects for 1941. "Even if the United States were our ally, instead of our friend and indispensable partner, we should not ask for a large American expeditionary army," Churchill wrote. He knew that, although Congress had passed the Selective Training and Service Act in September requiring all male US citizens between the ages of 21 and 35 to register for the draft, those drafted were only allowed to serve within US territories or possessions, or within the Western Hemisphere. Churchill wrote:

Shipping, not men, is the limiting factor. Unless we can establish our ability to feed this Island, to import the munitions of all kinds which we need, unless we can move our armies to the various theatres where Hitler and his confederate, Mussolini, must be met, and maintain them there, and do all this with the assurance of being able to carry it on till the spirit of the Continental Dictators is broken, we may fall by the way, and the time needed by the United States to complete her defensive preparations may not be forthcoming.

SHIPPING LOSSES

With the letter, Churchill sent the shipping losses for the past few months which had been "on a scale almost comparable to that of the worst years of the last war." He asked Roosevelt either to have American warships and aircraft escort merchant shipping, or give the British the ships to do it. He also pointed out that Britain was running out of money.

"The moment approaches when we shall no longer be able to pay cash for shipping and supplies," he wrote. If the trade were to cease, "not only should we in Great Britain suffer cruel privations but widespread unemployment in the United States would follow the curtailment of American exporting power."

Generosity by the American government would be approved and admired by future generations on both sides of the Atlantic. He concluded:

If, as I believe, you are convinced, Mr. President, that the defeat of the Nazi and Fascist tyranny is a matter of high consequence to the people of the United States and to the Western Hemisphere, you will regard this letter not as an appeal for aid, but as a statement of the minimum action necessary to the achievement of our common purpose.

Churchill later said that this was "one of the most important letters I ever wrote." Roosevelt was taking a short cruise in the Caribbean onboard the USS *Tuscaloosa*. Harry Hopkins saw him sitting in a deckchair re-reading Churchill's letter and brooding over it.

Roosevelt then proposed the concept of lend-lease. He told a press conference on December 17:

> *What I am trying to do is to eliminate the dollar sign … the silly, foolish old dollar sign. Well, let me give you an illustration: Suppose my neighbor's home catches fire, and I have a length of garden hose four or five hundred feet away. If he can take my garden hose and connect it up with his hydrant, I may help him to put out his fire. Now, what do I do? I don't say to him before that operation, "Neighbor, my garden hose cost me $15; you have to pay me $15 for it." What is the transaction that goes on? I don't want $15—I want my garden hose back after the fire is over. All right. If it goes through the fire all right, intact, without any damage to it, he gives it back to me and thanks me very much for the use of it. But suppose it gets smashed up—holes in it—during the fire; we don't have to have too much formality about it, but I say to him, "I was glad to lend you that hose; I see I can't use it any more, it's all smashed up." He says, "How many feet of it were there?" I tell him, "There were 150 feet of it." He says, "All right, I will replace it." Now, if I get a nice garden hose back, I am in pretty good shape.*
>
> *In other words, if you lend certain munitions and get the munitions back at the end of the war, if they are intact—haven't been hurt—you are all right; if they have been damaged or have deteriorated or have been lost completely, it seems to me you come out pretty well if you have them replaced by the fellow to whom you have lent them.*

But until the Lend-Lease Bill was passed by Congress, supplies still had to be paid for and a US warship was sent to pick up £30 million gold from South Africa.

LEND-LEASE

Congress passed the Lend-Lease Act on March 11, 1941. It gave the President the authority to aid any nation whose defense he believed was vital to the United States and to accept payment "in kind or property, or any other direct or indirect benefit which the President deems satisfactory." Principally enacted to aid Great Britain, it was extended to China in April and the Soviet Union in September. By the end of the war, more than forty nations were included in the program. Munitions and supplies worth over $50 billion ($682 billion today) were provided. Much of this was an outright gift, though some was offset by the $8 billion of aid provided by Allied nations to US troops stationed abroad.

Winston Churchill and US Ambassador John G. Winant signing the "Lend-Lease" agreement to lease British bases to America, March 11, 1941.

CHAPTER 8

THE ARSENAL OF DEMOCRACY

In his fireside chat of December 29, 1940, Roosevelt explained to radio listeners that America must be "the great arsenal of democracy." Specifically, he said: "We have furnished the British great material support and we will furnish far more in the future."

At Christmas, Roosevelt was still mulling over Churchill's letter and said to Harry Hopkins who was now living in the White House: "You know, a lot of this could be settled if Churchill and I could just sit down together for a while."

"What's stopping you?" Hopkins asked.

"Well it couldn't be arranged right now," said Roosevelt. "They have no Ambassador here, we have none over there."

"How about me going over, Mr. President?" said Hopkins.

Roosevelt dismissed the idea and remained obdurate. Then suddenly, without telling Hopkins, he announced at a press conference on January 3, that Hopkins would go to England "as my personal representative for a very short trip, a couple of weeks, just to maintain, I suppose that is the word for it, personal relations between me and the British Government."

THE PERFECT AMBASSADOR

It is unclear why Roosevelt took time to come round to the idea. He used to say: "Harry is the perfect ambassador for my purposes. He doesn't even know the meaning of the word 'protocol.' When he sees a piece of red tape, he just pulls out those old garden shears of his and snips it. And when he's talking to some foreign dignitary, he knows how to slump back in his chair and put his feet up on the conference table and say, 'Oh, yeah?'"

Neither Churchill nor the Foreign Office knew who Hopkins was. However the Prime Minister had been told that he was devoted to Roosevelt, and knew Hopkins was suspicious of anyone who might challenge Roosevelt's pre-eminence as a world statesman.

"Churchill is the British War Cabinet and no one else matters," Hopkins was told by Jean Monnet, a French banker with the British Purchasing Board in Washington.

"I suppose Churchill is convinced that he's the greatest man in the world," Hopkins shot back. There were still rumors, probably put about by Joseph Kennedy, that Churchill disliked Roosevelt and the United States, despite their cordial correspondence.

DAYS OF STRESS AND STORM

As Hopkins flew to England on January 9, 1941, Churchill did a little buttering up. He gave a speech at the Pilgrims, an Anglo-American society, at the Savoy Hotel, saying:

I have always taken the view that the fortunes of mankind in its tremendous journey are principally decided for good or ill—but mainly for good, for the path is upward—by its greatest men and its greatest episodes.

I therefore hail it as a most fortunate occurrence that at this awe-striking climax in world affairs there should stand at the head of the American Republic a famous statesman, long versed and experienced in the work of government and administration, in whose heart there burns the fire of resistance to aggression and oppression, and whose sympathies and nature make him the sincere and undoubted champion of justice and of freedom, and of the victims of wrongdoing wherever they may dwell.

WENDELL L. WILLKIE

After serving in the US Army during World War I, though he saw no action, Wendell Willkie (1892 – 1944) became a corporate lawyer and came to national prominence as head of the utility holding company Commonwealth & Southern in its legal battle against the Tennessee Valley Authority, set up by Roosevelt's administration to supply, among other things, electricity. A long-time Democratic Party activist, he changed his party registration to Republican in 1939. Although he did not run in the 1940 presidential primaries, when the convention was deadlocked, he gained the backing of uncommitted delegates and won the nomination over Thomas E. Dewey, an isolationist.

Willkie backed Roosevelt's policy of sending aid to Britain and the draft, removing them as campaign issues. Both men voiced isolationist sentiments toward the end of the race. Willkie won more than 22 million in the popular vote—the largest ever received by a Republican—but carried only ten states and 82 electoral votes against Roosevelt's 449.

He then stressed the need for a "loyal opposition" and supported Lend-Lease, alienating many Republicans. When he visited Roosevelt in the White House the evening before Roosevelt's swearing in, the President asked him to be an informal personal envoy to Britain and gave him a letter to hand to Churchill. He returned to Washington to testify before the Senate Foreign Relations Committee where his support was key to passing Lend-Lease. He then lobbied congressmen to repeal the Neutrality Act and visited the Soviet Union, the Middle East, and China for the President.

Willkie ran again for the Republican nomination in 1944, but withdrew from the race after a disastrous defeat in the Wisconsin primary.

JOSEPH P. KENNEDY

Rumored to have been a bootlegger during prohibition, Joseph Kennedy (1888 – 1969) was a bank president at age 25 and a millionaire by 30. A shipbuilder and a movie tycoon, he became a major contributor to the Democratic Party. In the bull market of the 1920s, he mastered the art of stock-exchange manipulation, retiring in 1929 before the Wall Street crash with enough money to set up a million-dollar trust fund for each of his nine children. Appointed chairman of the Securities and Exchange Commission by Roosevelt, he then outlawed the speculative practices that had made him rich. He went on to become chairman of the United States Maritime Commission, then in 1937 became the first Irish-American US Ambassador to Great Britain, quitting in November 1940 convinced both that Britain would lose the war to Nazi Germany and that America's only hope lay in isolationism. He was the father of the 35th US President John F. Kennedy.

And not less—for I may say it now that the party struggle in the United States is over—do I rejoice that this pre-eminent figure should newly have received the unprecedented honor of being called for the third time to lead the American democracies in days of stress and storm.

WHAT A MAN!

The following morning, after a briefing from US military and naval attachés, Hopkins was taken to the Foreign Office. At midday, he made his way to 10 Downing Street for lunch with the Prime Minister. Introducing himself to Churchill, Hopkins told him that the President had sent him to London "to tell you that at all costs and by all means he will carry you through, no matter what happens to him—there is nothing that he will not do so far as he has human power." The two talked until four o'clock in the morning.

Churchill said he immediately recognized "here was an envoy from the President of supreme importance to our life." He cabled Roosevelt saying: "I am most grateful to you for sending so remarkable an envoy who enjoys so high a measure of your intimacy and confidence."

When Hopkins brought up the matter of Churchill not liking America, Americans, or Roosevelt, Churchill reacted badly, as Hopkins recalled:

This set him off on a bitter tho' fairly constrained attack on Ambassador Kennedy who he believes is responsible for this impression. He denied it vigorously—sent for a Secretary to show me a telegram which he had sent to the President immediately after his election in which he expressed his warm delight at the President's re-election.

This was the telegram Roosevelt had not acknowledged.

Afterward Hopkins told US military attaché General Raymond E. Lee: "I have never had such an enjoyable time as I had with Mr. Churchill, but God, what a force that man has!" A few days later Hopkins repeated his star-struck admiration of Churchill to Viscount Lord Chandos a member of the War Cabinet declaring: "What a man!"

THIS ISLAND NEEDS OUR HELP

Churchill's assessment was that Hopkins was an "extraordinary man, who played, and was to play, a sometimes decisive part in the whole movement of the war."

They developed a close personal friendship and Hopkins was one of the few people who could prick the Prime Minister's pomposity without causing offense. On one occasion he interrupted Churchill in mid flow, saying: "Now, Mr. Prime Minister, I don't want a speech—I want something I can take back to convince the President you are right."

When asked by CBS London bureau chief Edward R. Murrow what he had come to do, Hopkins said: "I suppose you could say that I've come here to try to find a way to be a catalytic agent between two prima donnas. I want to try to get an understanding of Churchill and of the men he sees after midnight." Hopkins reported to Roosevelt:

Churchill wants to see you—the sooner the better—but I have told him of your problem until the bill is passed. I am convinced this meeting between you and Churchill is essential—and soon—for the battering continues and Hitler does not wait for Congress … I cannot believe that it is true that Churchill dislikes either you or America—it just doesn't make sense … This island needs our help now Mr. President with everything we can give them.

THE FOUR ESSENTIAL HUMAN FREEDOMS

Hopkins spent the weekend with Churchill, Clementine, and a handful of aids at Ditchley, an eighteenth-century house near Blenheim. Churchill read the text of the Lend-Lease Bill that had just been released and was delighted that it allowed British warships the use of

American ports and gave the President wide powers to assist. It was, he said, tantamount to a declaration of war, or at least an open challenge to Germany to declare war if she dared.

After dinner was over, Hopkins paid tribute to Churchill's speeches, saying they had "produced the most stirring and revolutionary effect on all classes and districts in America." Roosevelt had a radio brought into a cabinet meeting so he could listen to them.

Churchill then held forth, saying after the war "there must be a United States of Europe and he believed it should be built by the English; if the Russians built it, there would be communism and squalor; if the Germans built it, there would be tyranny and brute force."

Then he became high-flown and over the top:

> We seek no treasure, we seek no territorial gains, we seek only the right of man to be free; we seek his rights to worship his God, to lead his life in his own way, secure from persecution. As the humble laborer returns from his work when the day is done, and sees the smoke curling upwards from his cottage home in the serene evening sky, we wish him to know that no rat-a-tat-tat [here he rapped on the table] of the secret police upon his door will disturb his leisure or interrupt his rest. We seek government with the consent of the people, man's freedom to say what he will, and when he thinks himself injured, to find himself equal in the eyes of the law. But war aims other than these we have none.

Turning to Hopkins, Churchill asked: "What will the President say to all this?" For the best part of a minute, Hopkins remained silent. Then he said: "Well, Mr. Prime Minister, I don't think the President will give a damn for all that."

Then there was another long pause.

"You see, we're only interested in seeing that that goddamn sonofabitch Hitler gets licked."

There was laughter. Of course, Roosevelt did give a damn. Only a few days before in his State of the Union address he had expressed similar sentiments with his four freedoms:

> In the future days, which we seek to make secure, we look forward to a world founded upon four essential human freedoms.
>
> The first is freedom of speech and expression—everywhere in the world.
>
> The second is freedom of every person to worship God in his own way—everywhere in the world.
>
> The third is freedom from want—which, translated into world terms, means economic understandings which will secure to every nation a healthy peacetime life for its inhabitants—everywhere in the world.
>
> The fourth is freedom from fear—which, translated into world terms, means a world-wide reduction of armaments to such a point and in such a thorough fashion that no nation will be in a position to commit an act of physical aggression against any neighbor—anywhere in the world.

ALL THE HOPE OF FUTURE YEARS

Roosevelt wrote a letter to Churchill on January 20, 1941, with a verse from the Longfellow poem "The Building of the Ship." It was then hand-delivered to the British Prime Minister by Wendell Willkie, Roosevelt's Republican opponent in the 1940 Presidential election. Churchill, desperate for US support, said he found the letter "an inspiration" and told Roosevelt that he would have it framed. The letter hung for a long time at Chartwell, and the original green of White House stationery faded to brown:

> January 20, 1941
>
> Dear Churchill
>
> Wendell Willkie will give you this—He is truly helping to keep politics out over here.
> I think this verse applies to you people as it does to us:
>
> "Sail on, Oh Ship of State!
> Sail on, Oh Union strong and great.
> Humanity with all its fears
> With all the hope of future years
> Is hanging breathless on thy fate."
>
> As ever yours
> Franklin D. Roosevelt

CHARLES LINDBERGH

In 1927, 25-year-old Charles Augustus Lindbergh (1902 – 74) broke the record for the first non-stop solo transatlantic flight from New York to Paris in the purpose-built plane *Spirit of St. Louis*. He became an American hero overnight. But in 1932, tragically his young son was kidnapped and murdered. He and his wife fled into voluntary exile to escape hounding by the American press.

They began traveling in Europe, and Lindbergh accepted an invitation from Adolf Hitler to survey the might of the German air force. In 1938, after a number of visits to Nazi Germany, Hitler pushed Lindbergh's propaganda value to the limit by awarding him the Distinguished Service Cross of the German Eagle. The Lindberghs returned home in 1939.

After Hitler invaded Poland in 1939, Lindbergh began a campaign of radio broadcasts advocating that America should stay out of the fight. He said the German airpower he had seen with his own eyes was overwhelming. But Lindbergh refused to condemn Hitler's brutality toward the Jewish people, insisting there was violence on both sides. He came to be seen as a Nazi sympathizer.

In the summer of 1940, the America First Committee (AFC) was formed to maintain American neutrality. Lindbergh joined in 1941 and became spokesman. He toured around America speaking to thousands. Dorothy Thompson, Lindbergh's most vocal critic, wrote "this man has a notion to be our Fuehrer." People began to call for Lindbergh's name to be removed from street signs, and even William Hearst's pro-AFC newspapers began to denounce Lindbergh as un-American.

At its peak the AFC had more than 800,000 members including Walt Disney, Frank Lloyd Wright, and Henry Ford, but on December 7, 1941, the Japanese bombed Pearl Harbor and America entered World War II. The AFC was officially disbanded and Lindbergh finally pledged his support to the American war effort, flying fifty combat missions in the Pacific.

In his later years, Lindbergh became an author and environmentalist. He died in 1974 at age 72. Although he had six children with his wife Anne, in 2003 Lindbergh was revealed as the father of seven other children through secret extramarital affairs with three women in Europe.

AMERICA FIRST

Although the phrase "America First" had been around since the trade war with Britain in the late nineteenth century, the expression only became nationally popular when President Woodrow Wilson adopted America First as his catchphrase in April 1915.

Wilson had been president for three years when he made his initial America First speech, campaigning for re-election on the basis of keeping America out of World War I. Wilson claimed he was often misquoted and that his push for neutrality in the war was meant as a way of preparing to help both sides when the struggle was over. Fearing his message was being misunderstood, he warned the nation against news that turned out to be false—fake news.

Although seven presidents lobbied against lynching, Woodrow Wilson was not one of them, and he was not too troubled when his America First campaign became associated with racial purity. In 1915 Wilson became the first president to show a movie in the White House. He chose *The Birth of a Nation* directed by D.W. Griffith, a notoriously racist movie.

Based on *The Clansman,* a novel by Thomas H. Dixon, *The Birth of a Nation* was a national sensation at the time. However, the movie was entirely responsible for the revival of the Ku Klux Klan, prompting race riots and violence in cities and towns across America.

One hundred years later in 2016, Donald J. Trump became the 45th American president, resurrecting the phrase when he promised in his campaign speeches to put "America First."

FURY AND DEFIANCE

Harry Hopkins accompanied Churchill on a train journey to say farewell to Lord Halifax from Scapa Flow in the north of Scotland. He was traveling to Washington as British ambassador after the death of Lord Lothian.

At a small dinner party in the North British Hotel, Glasgow, Hopkins rose to propose a toast. "I suppose you wish to know what I am going to say to President Roosevelt on my return," he said. "Well I am going to quote to you one verse from the Book of Ruth ... 'Whither thou goest, I will go and where thou lodgest I will lodge, thy people shall be my people, and thy God my God.'"

Hopkins was also with Churchill at Chequers when the Prime Minister phoned the White House, saying: "Mr. President—it's me—Winston speaking."

One evening they were discussing American aviator Charles Lindbergh's call for a negotiated peace. In 1941, Lindbergh was the embodiment of the isolationist America First campaign, long before Donald Trump's recent revival. A negotiated peace, Churchill said "would be a German victory and leave open the way for another and final 'spring of the Tiger' in a few years' time ... Never give in and you will never regret it."

Agreeing, Hopkins said that Lindbergh and the America First Committee really wanted a German victory. Churchill wound up proceedings by saying that after the last war he had been asked to provide an inscription for a French war memorial. His suggestion, which was rejected, had been: "In war fury, in defeat defiance, in victory magnanimity, in peace good will."

GIVE US THE TOOLS

Hopkins was completely won over, but Churchill still had to work his magic on Roosevelt. As always, he had to walk a fine line, showing that Britain was not a lost cause but needed American help to win through. In his radio broadcast on February 9, 1941, Churchill said:

I have been so very careful, since I have been Prime Minister, not to encourage false hopes or prophesy smooth and easy things, and yet the tale that I have to tell today is one which must justly and rightly give us cause for deep thankfulness, and also, I think, for strong comfort and even rejoicing. But now I must dwell upon the more serious, darker and more dangerous aspects of the vast scene of the war. We must all of us have been asking ourselves: What has that wicked man whose crime-stained regime and system are at bay and in the toils—what has he been preparing during these winter months? What new devilry is he planning? What new small country will he overrun or strike down? What fresh form of assault will he make upon our island home and fortress? Which, let there be no mistake about it, is all that stands between him and the dominion of the world.

Winston Churchill touring a war-torn street in Bristol, after German bombers had raided the city in 1941.

He read the verse of Longfellow that Roosevelt had sent him: "Sail on, Oh Ship of State." Then he made a direct and flattering appeal to the President:

> What is the answer that I shall give, in your name, to this great man, the thrice-chosen head of a nation of a hundred and thirty millions? Here is the answer which I will give to President Roosevelt: Put your confidence in us. Give us your faith and your blessing, and, under Providence, all will be well.
>
> We shall not fail or falter; we shall not weaken or tire. Neither the sudden shock of battle, nor the long-drawn trials of vigilance and exertion will wear us down. Give us the tools, and we will finish the job.

THE BRILLIANT AND GREAT LEADER

When Hopkins returned to Washington, over lunch with the President, he suggested that, as Churchill made so many gracious references to him in the speeches, perhaps Roosevelt might return the compliment. So in a speech supporting the Lend-Lease Bill at the White House Correspondents Association annual dinner on March 15, Roosevelt said:

> The British people are braced for invasion whenever such attempt may come— tomorrow—next week—next month. In this historic crisis, Britain is blessed with a brilliant and great leader in Winston Churchill. But, knowing him, no one knows better than Mr. Churchill himself that it is not alone his stirring words and valiant deeds that give the British their superb morale. The essence of that morale is in the masses of plain people who are completely clear in their minds about the one essential fact—that they would rather die as free men than live as slaves.

When Roosevelt won the Lend-Lease vote on February 8, Hopkins tried to phone Churchill, but he was asleep. Instead he sent a message, saying: "… you and your country have innumerable friends here. I find my thoughts constantly with you in the desperate struggle which I am sure is going to result, in the last analysis, in your victory. Do remember me ever so cordially to Mrs. Churchill and Mary. I hope to send you some Victrola records in a few days and am on the trail of a Stilton cheese."

Churchill replied: "Thank God for your news. Strain is serious." And to Roosevelt, he wrote: "Our blessings from the whole of the British Empire go out to you and the American nation for this very present help in time of trouble."

PART THREE

THE GREATEST TWO MEN OF THE AGE

*To meet Roosevelt with all
his buoyant sparkle, his iridescence,
was like opening a bottle of champagne.*

Churchill about Roosevelt

CHAPTER 9

DELIGHTING IN SUBTERFUGE

After dinner on July 11, 1941, Roosevelt and Hopkins talked late into the night. On June 22, Hitler had torn up the German-Soviet Non-Agression Pact and launched an invasion of the USSR known as Operation Barbarossa. Now the US had the problem of supplying Russia as well. Hopkins was to fly to London to explain the situation and arrange for a shipboard meeting between Roosevelt and Churchill, their first since the beginning of the war. Secrecy was of the utmost importance.

Churchill was going to have to cross the Atlantic twice. It was teeming with German U-boats and he would also be very vulnerable to airborne attack part of the way. Secrecy was important for Roosevelt too. American isolationists were still strong and a meeting with Churchill would give them political ammunition.

Taking cheese, ham, and cigars for Churchill, Hopkins went to England. Churchill met him in the garden of 10 Downing Street.

RENDEZVOUS AT SEA

"We sat together in the sunshine," Churchill recalled. "Presently he said that the President would like very much to have a meeting with me in some lonely bay or other." That night they spoke to Roosevelt on the phone and everything was arranged.

It was very hot in Washington that summer and Roosevelt told the press that he was going to take a fishing trip off the coast of Maine "to get some cool nights." He boarded the presidential yacht *Potomac* at New London, Connecticut, in full view of a crowd of a

German infantry advance into Russia during Operation Barbarossa, 1941. The large Swastika sign serves as identification to the covering German aircraft from attacking their own troops.

thousand, then set sail with the presidential flag flying from the mast. They sailed to Martha's Vineyard where they met up with the heavy cruiser USS *Augusta* and Roosevelt transferred aboard in the middle of the night of August 3.

The chief of the White House Secret Services replaced him on board the *Potomac*, lounging on deck, flourishing Roosevelt's signature cigarette holder. Press releases about the fishing trip were issued. One said: "President spent quiet day. His Scotty Fala becoming restless for a little shore leave. All hands fishing." Roosevelt said he found this subterfuge "delightful." Meanwhile the *Augusta* headed for Newfoundland with an escort of a heavy cruiser and four destroyers. The presidential flag remained on the *Potomac* so it could be seen as it passed through the Cape Cod Canal.

PREPARING FOR GREAT EVENTS

After a quick trip to Moscow, Hopkins joined Churchill on board HMS *Prince of Wales*. One night as they crossed the Atlantic, they watched the movie *That Hamilton Woman* with Vivien Leigh playing Lady Hamilton and her husband Laurence Olivier playing Lord Nelson. Although it was the fifth time he had seen it, Churchill was moved to tears.

"Gentlemen, I thought this film would be of interest to you, showing great events, similar to those in which you have been taking part," he said.

It was certainly of interest to the isolationist America First Committee who tried to ban the film as it "seemed to be preparing Americans for war." Indeed, Churchill had contributed part of the script. The movie had been made in Hollywood and producer Alexander Korda was accused of providing propaganda for Britain in the US by the Senate Foreign Relations Committee. He escaped charges because his appearance before the committee, scheduled for December 12, 1941, was pre-empted by the attack on Pearl Habor.

On the morning of August 9, 1941, off Argentia in Placentia Bay, Newfoundland, where America was building a seaplane station under the terms of the destroyers-for-bases deal, the *Prince of Wales* came alongside the *Augusta* with Old Glory flying above it. While the band of the Royal Marines played "The Star-Spangled Banner," the *Augusta* resounded to the tune of "God Save The King."

Churchill, dressed in the blue uniform of the Warden of the Cinque Ports, crossed to the American flagship and mounted the gangway. Roosevelt was wearing a tan Palm Beach suit and had donned leg braces so he could stand to greet his guest. They were painful and the slight pitch of the *Augusta* meant he risked a humiliating fall, so he braced himself on the arm of his son Elliott.

"We've got to make it clear," Roosevelt told his son, "that from the very outset we don't intend to be simply a good-time Charlie who can be used to help the British Empire out of a tight spot and then to be forgotten forever."

WARMEST OF WELCOMES

Churchill seized the opportunity to flash a V for Victory sign. Then, with a slight bow, Churchill presented Roosevelt with a letter from King George VI, introducing him. It said: "How glad I am that you have the opportunity at last of getting to know my Prime Minister. I am sure you will agree that he is a very remarkable man."

Churchill said he received "the warmest of welcomes."

As they shook hands, Roosevelt said: "At last, we've gotten together."

"We have," said Churchill with a nod.

Over lunch, Roosevelt reminded Churchill that they had met before—at the dinner in Gray's Inn in 1918. Churchill had no recollection of the event, but pretended he did in the most flattering terms, saying in his memoirs: "I had been struck by his magnificent presence in all his youth and strength." Though irked, Roosevelt overlooked the deception. It was vital to get the summit off to a good start. According to Elliott Roosevelt: "It didn't take them long, talking about their correspondence, their transatlantic phone conversations, their

THE TRIPARTITE PACT

The Tripartite Pact, also known as the Berlin Pact, was an agreement between Germany, Italy, and Japan signed in Berlin on September 27, 1940. Directed primarily as a statement of intent against the United States, its practical effects were limited, since the Italo-German axis and Japanese operations were on opposite sides of the world.

A 1941 propaganda poster created to strengthen the pact between Japan, Germany, and Italy.

health, their jobs and their worries, to be calling each other 'Franklin' and 'Winston.'"

Eager to find out how he had done with Roosevelt, Churchill later asked Averell Harriman: "Does he like me?" Harriman assured him it had gone well.

Roosevelt said of his first impression: "He is a tremendously vital person & in many ways is an English Mayor La Guardia [Fiorello H. La Guardia, the charismatic 99th mayor of New York City] and lunching alone broke the ice both ways." In his turn, Roosevelt asked his aides: "What did he think of me?"

FIXING THE FAR EAST

At 6:45 p.m., Churchill and his party returned to the *Augusta* for dinner. Roosevelt talked about the Christmas trees he was growing at Hyde Park which he hoped to sell when the holiday approached. Then the conversation turned to the situation in the Far East.

During the 1920s, the power of the Japanese military had grown and the country veered toward Fascism and expansionism. In 1931, Japan invaded Manchuria. It had quit the League of Nations in 1933 and in 1936 signed the Anti-Comintern Pact with Germany. The following year Japan began its invasion of China, then in 1940 signed the Tripartite Pact with Germany and Italy, making it one of the Axis powers. A brief border war in Manchuria led to a Soviet-Japanese Neutrality Pact, which held until August 9, 1945—the day the second atomic bomb was dropped on Nagasaki.

After the fall of France, Japan invaded French Indo-China—modern day Vietnam, Laos, and Cambodia. In response, the US halted shipments of airplanes, parts, machine tools, and aviation gasoline to Japan. Britain feared for her colonies in Asia, particularly Hong Kong, Malaya, and Singapore.

Early in 1941, President Roosevelt ordered a military build-up in the Philippines, then in July the US imposed an oil embargo on Japan. When Roosevelt returned to Washington on August 17, he warned the Japanese that the US was prepared to take steps against Japan if it attacked "neighboring countries." However,

negotiations to improve relations between the US and Japan continued throughout 1941.

CHURCHILL HOLDS FORTH

Over dinner, Roosevelt also mentioned that it might be a good idea if he and Churchill drew up a joint declaration laying down certain broad principles to guide their policies down the same road. However it was Churchill who dominated the conversation. Elliott Roosevelt recalled:

At dinner, and afterwards, too, as the evening wore on toward midnight, I saw Father in a new role. My experience of him in the past had been that he dominated every gathering he was part of; not because he insisted on it so much as that it always seemed his natural due. But not tonight. Tonight Father listened. Somebody else was holding the audience, holding it with grand, roiling, periodic speeches, never quite too florid, always ripe and fruity to the point where it seemed you'd be able to take his sentences in your hands and squeeze them until the juice ran out. Winston Churchill held every one of us, that night— and was conscious every second of the time that he was holding us. All that Father did was to throw in an occasional question—just drawing him on, drawing him out.

Other observers said Churchill was not even at his best that night. Acknowledging the political difficulties the US would have in sending troops, he again only asked Roosevelt for material aid. Churchill also said that the British needed bombers to bring home to the Germans the horrors of war, just as the Germans had brought it home to the British with the Blitz.

He pointed out that British policies from now on would be to attack the Germans at all points and that in the areas where the Germans had long-extended lines of communication the British would meet them on even terms. By constant hammering, it was possible to prevent the German army from spreading out any further, and the British attacks should ultimately aid in breaking Germany's morale.

ONWARD CHRISTIAN SOLDIERS!

The following day, August 10, was a Sunday and there was to be a church parade onboard the *Prince of Wales*. Churchill planned every detail. Roosevelt and Churchill would sit next to a lectern draped in the Union Jack and the Stars and Stripes, with the top officers and advisors behind them.

Roosevelt was to be ferried over by the destroyer USS *McDougal*. He would be wearing his leg braces again and there was a fear that, if he fell into the sea, he would sink to the bottom before he could be rescued. The *McDougal* set off from the *Augusta* with Roosevelt onboard at 10:30 a.m. and halted alongside the *Prince of Wales*, bow to stern,

starboard side to starboard side. The *Prince of Wales*'s crane was then used to hoist the President from one vessel to the other.

With one hand on the rail, the other holding Elliott's arm, Roosevelt walked toward Churchill while the Royal Marines formed an honor guard. Churchill then accompanied him as he made the taxing journey from the rail to his chair—"every step causing him pain," Churchill noted.

The service began with the hymn "O God, Our Help In Ages Past." After the General Confession and the Lord's Prayer, they sang "Onward, Christian Soldiers," which left Churchill in tears. There was a reading from the Book of Joshua, calling on them to "be strong and of good courage." Then there were prayers, including one saying: "We fight, not

President Roosevelt and Prime Minister Churchill seated on the quarterdeck of HMS *Prince of Wales* for a Sunday service during the Atlantic Conference, August 10, 1941.

in enmity against men, but against the powers of darkness enslaving the souls of men …" The service ended with the hymn "For Those In Peril On The Sea."

Roosevelt told his son afterward: "If nothing else had happened while we were here, that would have cemented us. 'Onward, Christian Soldiers' —we are, and we will go on, with God's help."

FIGHTING FOR OUR LIVES

After the church service Churchill gave Roosevelt what he called "a tentative outline of such a declaration" as he had asked for the day before. Photographs were taken. Roosevelt then reverted to his wheelchair for a tour of the ship. Ramps had been laid for ease of access.

Lunch followed. Churchill had insisted on serving grouse as he knew Roosevelt loved game. Roosevelt got more of the floor this time. He was "awfully good," said one British observer, "just like his fireside chats." That afternoon, Churchill pressed Roosevelt to take a tougher line with Japan.

The two men were more impressed with each other than ever.

"Great things may come of it in the future," Churchill told the officers around him. "You have seen a great man today."

Then it was time for a little relaxation.

"On this lovely day," Churchill said, "it is difficult to realize that we are fighting for our lives."

With three others Churchill went ashore, clambered up a cliff and insisted on rolling boulders down from the top of it. He talked incessantly, not even halting when it began to rain. They returned to the *Prince of Wales* with a bunch of wild flowers.

THE GREATEST MEN ON EARTH

That evening Churchill and Roosevelt had dinner together again. This time they had a disagreement. Churchill was fighting to preserve the British Empire. As a follower of Woodrow Wilson, Roosevelt supported self-determination and sought to improve the conditions of colonial peoples.

Even so, after dinner, Roosevelt told Churchill's bodyguard Inspector Thompson: "Look after the Prime Minister. He is one of the greatest men in the world."

There seems to have been a competition about who admired who more.

When Franklin Jr. accompanied Churchill back to the *Prince of Wales*, the Prime Minister said: "Your father is a great man … He has certainly had much to get through. And to get over."

"That is it," said Franklin Jr. "He has been determined to get over his affliction, and has done so."

Churchill went further.

"It is my opinion," he said, "that your father is one of the greatest men on the earth today."

Franklin Jr. smiled and said: "Father was talking to me of you while you were out of the dining room yesterday and said that Churchill …"

"No, no! Never that," said Churchill. "Winston. Winston. Your father always calls me Winston. He's never to do anything else!"

"Correct, sir," Franklin Jr. continued. "In any case, he said quite plainly and without reservation that you are the greatest statesman the world has ever known."

"I do not think of myself this way," said Churchill. "I'm just in the flood of the circumstance." [Elsewhere, Churchill referred to himself as "a dead cat floating on the sea, but would be eventually washed up on the shores of victory."]

"But the world thinks of you this way, Mr. Churchill," Franklin Jr. said. "So does my father. I told him that history would have time to make these evaluations but meantime it was my own evaluation that he, meaning my father, and you, sir, were certainly the greatest two men of the age and that together you can bring peace to the world and keep it here."

CHAPTER 10

THE ATLANTIC ALLIANCE

The following morning, Roosevelt gave Churchill the amended text of their draft declaration. Before examining it, Churchill suggested that on August 14 a short statement about their discussions at sea should be issued simultaneously in Washington and London. These should be confined to the aid provided under the Lend-Lease Act and should not concern any future commitments, other than those authorized by Congress. However, the absence of commitment should not be stressed as it would be seized on by Germany causing profound discouragement among neutrals and the vanquished. Roosevelt accepted this.

Churchill suggested further alterations to the draft. He then telegraphed the Cabinet in London, who came up with more amendments. Roosevelt accepted all these. Churchill was delighted, and he wrote:

The fact alone of the United States, still technically neutral, joining with a belligerent power in making such a declaration is astonishing. The inclusion in it of a reference to "the final destruction of the Nazi tyranny" (this was based on a phrase appearing in my original draft) amounts to a challenge which in ordinary times would imply warlike action. Finally, not the least striking feature is the realism of the last paragraph where there is a plain and bold intimation that, after the war, the United States will join with us in policing the world until the establishment of a better order.

PARALLEL COMMUNICATIONS

After the church parade onboard the *Prince of Wales* Churchill also handed Roosevelt a short memorandum proposing a system of "parallel" communications to the Japanese government.

He proposed the US government make a declaration saying:

1. Any further encroachment by Japan in the South-West Pacific would produce a situation in which the United States Government would be compelled to take counter-measures even though these might lead to war between the United States and Japan.

2. If any third power becomes the object of aggression by Japan in consequence of such counter-measures or of their support of them, the President would have the intention to seek authority from Congress to give aid to such power.

The British government would make a similar declaration with the last paragraph amended to say "… their support of them. His Majesty's Government would give all possible aid to such power." The Dutch government in exile in London would issue a similar declaration. Churchill suggested that the Soviet government be kept informed and possibly pressed to make a similar declaration.

Churchill and Roosevelt discussed these proposals the following morning. Roosevelt said that he could not give an assurance that he would go to Congress for the authority to give armed support as negotiations were underway. He had received an assurance from the Japanese that they would station no further troops in the south-west Pacific area and ultimately withdraw those already in French Indo-China. Roosevelt said he was under no illusion about the value or sincerity of these assurances, but he thought it would be useful to continue discussions in the hope of gaining a month to make preparations.

THE ATLANTIC CHARTER

The Atlantic Charter set the guidelines for what would later become the United Nations. The official text of the Atlantic Charter was signed by President Franklin D. Roosevelt and Prime Minister Winston Churchill on August 14, 1941, aboard ship in Placentia Bay, Newfoundland.

The President of the United States and the Prime Minister, Mr. Churchill, representing H.M. Government in the United Kingdom, being met together, deem it right to make known certain common principles in the national policies of their respective countries on which they base their hopes for a better future for the world.

1. Their countries seek no aggrandizement, territorial or other.

2. They desire to see no territorial changes that do not accord with the freely expressed wishes of the peoples concerned.

3. They respect the right of all peoples to choose the form of Government under which they will live; and they wish to see sovereign rights and self-government restored to those who have been forcibly deprived of them.

4. They will endeavor, with due respect for their existing obligations, to further the enjoyment by all States, great or small, victor or vanquished, of access, on equal terms, to the trade and to the raw materials of the world which are needed for their economic prosperity.

5. They desire to bring about the fullest collaboration between all nations in the economic field, with the object of securing for all improved labor standards, economic advancement, and social security.

6. After the final destruction of the Nazi tyranny, they hope to see established a peace which will afford to all nations the means of dwelling in safety within their own boundaries, and which will afford assurance that all the men in all the lands may live out their lives in freedom from fear and want.

7. Such a peace should enable all men to traverse the high seas and oceans without hindrance.

8. They believe that all of the nations of the world, for realistic as well as spiritual reasons, must come to the abandonment of the use of force. Since no future peace can be maintained if land, sea, or air armaments continue to be employed by nations which threaten, or may threaten, aggression outside of their frontiers, they believe, pending the establishment of a wider and permanent system of general security, that the disarmament of such nations is essential. They will likewise aid and encourage all other practicable measures which will lighten for peace-loving peoples the crushing burden of armament.

Franklin D. Roosevelt and Winston Churchill after the signing of the Atlantic Charter.

TAKING COUNTER-MEASURES

Roosevelt's Under Secretary of State Sumner Welles thought that the time for warnings had run out. Churchill pointed out that it was clearly Japan's intention to attack Yunnan northward from Indo-China and cut the Burma Road—the Chinese supply route. A condition of continuing discussions, Churchill said, was that Indo-China should not be used as a base for operations against China.

Roosevelt agreed and said that when discussions resumed he would press for the neutralization of Siam (Thailand) and Indo-China. Furthermore, he would end his message to the Japanese ambassador with the words that Churchill had given him the day before—that any further encroachment by Japan "would produce a situation in which the United States Government would be compelled to take counter-measures even though these might lead to war between the United States and Japan."

He would add that, as the Soviet Union was now a friendly power, the US government would also have an interest in any conflict in the north-west Pacific area. Churchill then authorized the President to inform Japan that in this matter His Majesty's Government were in accord with the United States Government and would cooperate fully with them.

A CONSIDERABLE DETERRENT

Later Churchill asked for a copy of the message, but was told that it had not yet been drafted. However, Roosevelt assured him on several occasions that he would include the final words that Churchill had asked for. Churchill wrote:

> *I am confident that the President will not tone it down. He has a copy of the record of our conversation in which this wording is reproduced. Mr. Sumner Welles undertook that a copy of the draft of the message would be given as soon as possible to His Majesty's Ambassador in Washington. Even taken by itself this warning should have a considerable deterrent effect on Japan. And when we remember that the Japanese will already have suffered the shock of the Anglo-American joint declaration, I think we may hope that they will pause before proceeding to further outrage.*

Roosevelt said he was also expecting the Germans to move into the Iberian Peninsula around September 15. After making token resistance, the Portuguese government said it would withdraw to the Azores. He wanted Churchill to say that the British could not help defend the islands as they were busy elsewhere and tell the Portuguese Prime Minister Doctor Salazar to ask the United States instead.

The Presidential yacht *Potomac*, carrying Franklin Roosevelt, returns to Rockland, Maine, after the Atlantic Conference.

Roosevelt could then send troops to the Azores, along with a token force from Brazil, but not the Cape Verde Islands, also a Portuguese possession, as the Azores were within the neutral zone, which he now maintained included the entire western half of the Atlantic. The US Navy would also be sending ships to escort North Atlantic convoys there, assisted by the Royal Canadian Navy. The Royal Navy could then be deployed elsewhere.

The Cape Verde Islands would be a British responsibility and the Americans wanted the British to leave sufficient troops in Iceland, so that US Marines could be withdrawn. The Americans thought that the Germans would move down through Spain into North and West Africa. Studies had been made of possible operations in Morocco and Dakar in Senegal. The US was also preparing to occupy key points in South America and lease a base in Brazil because of active German organizations there.

Roosevelt told Churchill he would ask Congress for another $5 billion in Lend-Lease aid and together they would send a message to Stalin concerning the Soviet Union's need for aid.

FULL HONORS FOR CHURCHILL

On their last evening together, they talked about everything except the war. Churchill said it was the nicest evening he had had. He was accorded full honors as he left the *Augusta*. But he had something more valuable—more valuable even than the firm friendship of a man who had once kept him at bay. Roosevelt had told him privately: "I do not intend to declare war; I intend to wage it."

Back onboard the *Potomac* at Rockland, Maine, Roosevelt held a press conference on August 16. Clearly he had to guard his words as he still had Congress and public opinion to contend with. He told reporters:

The easiest thing to do is to give you what we might call the impressions that stand out. I

think the first thing in the minds of all of us was a very remarkable religious service on the quarterdeck of the Prince of Wales last Sunday morning. There was their own ship's complement, with three or four hundred bluejackets and marines from American ships, on the quarterdeck, completely intermingled, first one uniform and then another uniform … They had three hymns that everybody took part in, and a little ship's altar was decked with the American flag and the British flag. The officers were all intermingled on the fantail, and I think the pictures of it have been released. The point is, I think everybody there, officers and enlisted men, felt that it was one of the great historic services. I know I did.

Asked whether he could tell them anything about the implementation of the broad declarations in the Atlantic Charter, Roosevelt said it was an "interchange of views, that's all."

"Are we any closer to entering the war, actually?" he was asked.

"I should say, no."

Churchill and the British cabinet were unhappy when they heard this, and Churchill sent a cable to Hopkins:

I ought to tell you that there has been a wave of depression through Cabinet and other informed circles here about the President's many assurances about no commitments and no closer to war. If 1942 opens with Russia knocked out and Britain left again alone, all kinds of dangers may arise. I do not think Hitler will help in any way.

A MORE DEVELOPED MIND

Back in Washington, Roosevelt told his cabinet that he liked Churchill very much. Comparing the man he had met with the one he had previously disliked, he said: "His mind is improving. I'm sure that he's got a greater mind than he had twenty years ago. He's got a more developed mind."

Frances Perkins who was at the cabinet meeting said: "I remember being very, very glad that the President had liked Churchill and feeling that it was much safer for this country,

THE GREATEST TWO MEN OF THE AGE

as well as for the world, if President Roosevelt liked and was able to make rapprochement with Churchill, able to believe him, able to take some leadership from him."

This was because "Churchill has much more life experience of war, rumors of war, making war, making peace, keeping the world on an even keel than anybody in the USA did, including Franklin D. Roosevelt … I thought the whole relationship with Churchill was very, very lucky."

Roosevelt now had confidence in the Prime Minister. "You talked with Churchill," he told the cabinet, "and you understood the stubborn fight they were putting up and would continue to put up." However, he admitted to Eleanor that he did find Churchill "overpowering."

MARSHALING GOOD AGAINST EVIL

In his radio broadcast on August 24, 1941, Churchill was still ebullient, saying:

I thought you would like me to tell you something about the voyage which I made across the ocean to meet our great friend, the President of the United States. Exactly where we met is a secret, but I don't think I shall be indiscreet if I go so far as to say that it was somewhere in the Atlantic. In a spacious, land-locked bay which reminded me of the west coast of Scotland, powerful American warships, protected by strong flotillas and far-ranging aircraft, awaited our arrival and, as it were, stretched out a hand to help us in.

Our party arrived in the newest, or almost the newest, British battleship, the Prince of Wales, with a modest escort of British and Canadian destroyers. And there for three days I spent my time in company, and I think I may say in comradeship, with Mr. Roosevelt, while all the time the chiefs of the staff and naval and military commanders, both of the British Empire and of the United States, sat together in continual council.

President Roosevelt is the thrice-chosen head of the most powerful State and community

in the world. I am the servant of King and Parliament, at present charged with the principal direction of our affairs in these fateful times. And it is my duty also to make sure, as I have made sure, that anything I say or do in the exercise of my office is approved and sustained by the whole British Commonwealth of Nations. Therefore this meeting was bound to be important because of the enormous forces, at present only partially mobilized, but steadily mobilizing, which are at the disposal of these two major groupings of the human family, the British Empire and the United States, who, fortunately for the progress of mankind, happen to speak the same language and very largely think the same thoughts, or anyhow, think a lot of the same thoughts.

The meeting was, therefore, symbolic. That is its prime importance. It symbolizes, in a form and manner which every one can understand in every land and in every clime, the deep underlying unities which stir and, at decisive moments, rule the English-speaking peoples throughout the world. Would it be presumptuous for me to say that it symbolizes something even more majestic, namely, the marshaling of the good forces of the world against the evil forces which are now so formidable and triumphant and which have cast their cruel spell over the whole of Europe and a large part of Asia?

ATLANTIC RATTLESNAKES

On Thursday, September 4, 1941, German submarine U-652 mistakenly fired torpedoes at the USS *Greer*, an American destroyer. Churchill wondered whether this could be the incident that drew America into the war when Roosevelt cabled him saying: "For your private and very confidential information I am planning to make a radio address Monday night relative to the attack on our destroyer and to make perfectly clear the action we intend to take in the Atlantic."

However, Roosevelt was summoned to Hyde Park and that Sunday his mother Sara died.

He was with her. Churchill sent a telegram of condolence. His fireside chat was postponed until September 11 and he put down a marker:

> *We have sought no shooting war with Hitler. We do not seek it now. But neither do we want peace so much, that we are willing to pay for it by permitting him to attack our naval and merchant ships while they are on legitimate business … But when you see a rattlesnake poised to strike, you do not wait until he has struck before you crush him. These Nazi submarines and raiders are the rattlesnakes of the Atlantic … But let this warning be clear. From now on, if German or Italian vessels of war enter the waters, the protection of which is necessary for American defense, they do so at their own peril.*

Churchill, who had listened to the broadcast, wrote to a fellow former cadet, saying: "Roosevelt this morning was excellent. As we used to sing at Sandhurst 'Now we shan't be long!'"

WAR WITH JAPAN

After Thanksgiving Roosevelt went to Warm Springs, Georgia, which he had first visited when recuperating from polio, only to return quickly after receiving a call from Secretary of State Cordell Hull. Relations with Japan were reaching crisis point. During lunch at Chequers on December 7, the day of the Japanese attack on Pearl Harbor, Churchill asked US Ambassador John Gilbert Winant if he thought there would be a war with Japan.

Winant said: "Yes."

"If they declare war on you," Churchill reassured him, "we shall declare war on them within the hour."

The following day, after Britain's own Far East possessions had been attacked, that's what he did. Then as if to symbolize a personal attack on Churchill and Roosevelt, Japanese aircraft sunk the *Prince of Wales* and the battlecruiser HMS *Repulse* in the South China Sea on December 10. Nearly half of the men who had attended the church parade in Placentia Bay were now dead.

Franklin D. Roosevelt at the White House in Washington, delivering a national radio address on September 11, 1941. His black arm band is worn as a mark of respect for the death of his mother.

CHAPTER 11

TURNING THE TIDE IN NORTH AFRICA

As the Japanese made rapid advances in the Far East, German forces in North Africa under Erwin Rommel were also advancing. On January 29, 1942, Churchill faced a vote of no confidence in the House of Commons. In the debate he compared his precarious position with that of the leader in the US, saying:

Even in the great democracy of the United States the Executive does not stand in the same direct, immediate, day-to-day relation to the legislative body as we do. The President, in many vital respects independent of the legislature, Commander-in-Chief of all the Forces of the Republic, has a fixed term of office, during which his authority can scarcely be impugned. But here in this country the House of Commons is master all the time of the life of the administration.

He won by 464 votes to one. Roosevelt cabled Churchill: "Congratulations on yesterday's vote. We also had one vote in opposition."

Nevertheless, with Britain still in retreat everywhere, Churchill faced another vote of no confidence on July 2. Again he made American comparisons. Assessing the situation he said:

A peace-loving nation like the United States, confined by two great oceans, naturally takes time to bring its gigantic forces to bear. I have never shared the view that this would be a short war, or that it would end in 1942. It is far more likely to be a long war. There is no reason to suppose that the war will stop when the final result has become obvious. The Battle of Gettysburg proclaimed the ultimate victory of the North, but far more blood was shed after the Battle of Gettysburg than before.

This time he won by 475 to 25.

VALLEY FORGE

Roosevelt also turned to American history for succor in his broadcast commemorating George Washington's birthday on February 23, saying:

For eight years, General Washington and his Continental Army were faced continually with formidable odds and recurring defeats. Supplies and equipment were lacking. In a sense, every winter was a Valley Forge. Throughout the thirteen states there existed fifth columnists—and selfish men, jealous men, fearful men, who proclaimed that Washington's cause was hopeless, and that he should ask for a negotiated peace. Washington's conduct in those hard times has provided the model for all Americans ever since—a model of moral stamina. He held to his course, as it had been charted in the Declaration of Independence. He and the brave men who served with him knew that no man's life or fortune was secure without freedom and free institutions.

The fact that Washington was fighting against the British was quietly overlooked, though Roosevelt did quote English revolutionary Thomas Paine, saying: "Tyranny, like hell, is not easily conquered, yet we have this consolation with us, that the harder the sacrifice, the more glorious the triumph."

Churchill called the speech "heartening." And heartening was what he needed. Singapore had fallen to the Japanese a week before. With some 80,000 British, Australian, and Indian troops taken prisoner, Churchill called it the worst disaster in British military history. In a radio address trying to ameliorate the situation, Churchill mentioned that American sea power had been "dashed to the ground" at Pearl Harbor. Washington insiders were outraged. Was Churchill blaming the US Navy for the fall of Singapore?

"Winston has to say something," Roosevelt told those who complained and immediately picked up his pen to send Churchill a note saying:

> *I realize how the fall of Singapore has affected you and the British people. It gives the well-known back seat drivers a field day but no matter how serious our setbacks have been, and I do not for a moment underrate them, we must constantly look forward to the next moves that need to be made to hit the enemy. I hope you will be of good heart in these trying weeks because I am very sure that you have the great confidence of the masses of the British people. I want you to know that I think of you often and I know you will not hesitate to ask me if there is anything you think I can do.*

MISFORTUNES THICK AND FAST

The stress was getting to Churchill and he told Roosevelt that he "found it difficult to keep my eye on the ball."

Churchill remained disconsolate. He had always believed that the United States coming into the war would be Britain's savior, but now it was still suffering grave reverses.

"Misfortunes will come thick and fast upon us," he told Roosevelt.

"This may be a critical period," Roosevelt replied, "but remember always it is not as bad as some you have so well survived."

Roosevelt was soon bolstered on June 6, 1942, by victory at the Battle of Midway which destroyed much of the Japanese Fleet that had attacked Pearl Harbor and effectively ended any further Japanese encroachment in the Pacific.

There was unrest in Churchill's household when his son Randolph discovered his wife Pamela was having an affair with Averell Harriman and accused his parents of colluding in it. Roosevelt warmed to Pamela when he learned that she was one of the most beautiful women in London and longed to meet her.

Meanwhile Pamela kept a portrait of Roosevelt next to one of Churchill in her drawing room. Roosevelt and Churchill not only shared each other's problems concerning their children—Roosevelt had five, Churchill four and both had lost one early on—but also shared the delight they felt in their grandchildren. They both had boys in uniform which greatly concerned them.

Pamela Churchill with her son Winston Churchill Junior, April 1941.

FEARING A BLOODBATH

Roosevelt and his advisors were keen to land an Allied Force in France to attack Hitler's fortress Europe directly and take the pressure off the Russians. Churchill feared a bloodbath. He and Roosevelt also argued over India. Roosevelt thought that India should be self-governing, while for Churchill it was the jewel in the crown of the British Empire.

Churchill cabled Roosevelt: "Anything like a serious difference between you and me would break my heart, and would surely deeply injure both our countries at the height of this terrible struggle."

That laid the matter to rest for the moment, but they still had to decide what to do in the Western theater of the war. This meant that Churchill and Roosevelt would have to have another face-to-face meeting. On June 17, Churchill took a flying boat from Stranraer in Scotland to Washington. When he arrived, Roosevelt was at Hyde Park, while Eleanor was sorting out his late mother's possessions.

Two days later, Churchill flew up to New Hackensack airport near Hyde Park.

"The President was on the local airfield, and saw us make the roughest bump landing I have experienced," he recalled.

Roosevelt drove him around to see "the majestic bluffs over the Hudson River on which Hyde Park, his family home, stand" in his blue Ford that had been modified with hand levers replacing foot pedals. Churchill said:

> *An ingenious arrangement enabled him to do everything with his arms, which were amazingly strong and muscular. He invited me to feel his biceps, saying a famous prizefighter had envied them. This was reassuring; but I confess that when on several occasions the car poised and backed on the grass verges of the precipices over the Hudson I hoped the mechanical devices and brakes would show no defects. All the time we talked business, and though I was careful not to take his attention off the driving we made more progress than we might have done in a formal conference.*

Later that day, Churchill convinced Roosevelt that no responsible authority had been able to make a case for a landing in France in September 1942. To take the pressure off the Soviet Union, they should study the operation against French North Africa.

COUSIN DAISY

Churchill was impressed with Roosevelt's house. He was given a tour. Coming down the stairs he found Margaret "Daisy" Suckley, a cousin and intimate confidante of Roosevelt's, alone in the front hall. Churchill grew shy.

"Seeing a strange woman, he stopped on the lower stair landing and examined a painting," Daisy recalled. "I started to gaze at something, too—it may have been the trees. He turned and came down the last two steps. He smiled, I smiled. We shook hands. I introduced myself. We wandered down the hall to the library."

Later watching Roosevelt and Churchill together, she noted:

FDR snapped this photo of Daisy Suckley as she worked on his family archives in the White House, February 10, 1942.

*There seemed to be real friendship &
understanding between F.D.R. and
Churchill. F.D.R.'s manner was easy and
intimate—His face humorous, or very serious,
according to the subject of conversation,
and entirely natural. Not a trace of having
to guard his words or expressions, just the
opposite of his manner at a press conference,
when he is an actor on a stage—and a player
on an instrument, at the same time.*

TUBE ALLOYS

Roosevelt asked Daisy to arrange tea at Top
Cottage the next day. She should lay on Scotch
and ice too, in case Churchill wanted some.
Before they left Hyde Park, they discussed
a project the British code named "Tube
Alloys"—the making of an atomic bomb.
The idea that you could make an atomic
bomb came from Leo Szilard, a Hungarian
physicist who had fled to London to escape
the Nazis. Later he moved to the US where
he visited his old colleague Albert Einstein—

they had previously worked together in Berlin.
They wrote a letter to the President, signed
by Einstein, telling him of the possibility of
making an atomic bomb and warning him that
the Germans could be building one.

Roosevelt's response was to set up a
committee to study the feasibility of making
such a device. They were skeptical about the
possibilities of making a bomb, especially as it
would be hugely expensive, until they received
a report from Britain that contained a specific
plan to build a bomb small enough to be
loaded on to an existing aircraft that could be
ready in, perhaps, as little as two years. Britain
did not have the resources to make the bomb,
nor the facilities which would be safe from
conventional bombing.

"I strongly urged that we should at once
pool all our information, work together on
equal terms, and share the results, if any,
equally between us," Churchill said. Roosevelt
agreed that they should push ahead and the
British scientists were sent to work in America
on what became known as the Manhattan
Project.

Albert Einstein (left) and Leo Szilard in 1939.

MADISON SQUARE GARDEN RALLY

On July 21, 1942, Jewish organizations held a rally at Madison Square Garden to protest the Nazis' treatment of Jews. Both Roosevelt and Churchill sent statements to be read out there.

ROOSEVELT'S STATEMENT

Americans who love justice and hate oppression will hail the solemn commemoration in Madison Square Garden as an expression of the determination of the Jewish people to make every sacrifice for victory over the Axis powers. Citizens, regardless of religious allegiance, will share in the sorrow of our Jewish fellow-citizens over the savagery of the Nazis against their helpless victims. The Nazis will not succeed in exterminating their victims any more than they will succeed in enslaving mankind. The American people not only sympathize with all victims of Nazi crimes but will hold the perpetrators of these crimes to strict accountability in a day of reckoning which will surely come.

I express the confident hope that the Atlantic Charter and the just world order made possible by the triumph of the United Nations will bring the Jews and oppressed people in all lands the four freedoms which Christian and Jewish teachings have largely inspired.

CHURCHILL'S STATEMENT

You are meeting this evening to condemn Hitler's atrocities in Europe and to offer all assistance to the United Nations in the war on the Axis. You will recall that on October 25 last year both President Roosevelt and I expressed the horror felt by all civilized peoples at Nazi butcheries and terrorism and our resolve to place retribution for these crimes among the major purposes of this war. The Jews were Hitler's first victims, and ever since they had been in the forefront of resistance to Nazi aggression.

All over the world Jewish communities have made their contribution to the cause of the United Nations and on behalf of His Majesty's Government in the United Kingdom I welcome your determination to help as gladly as I acknowledge the eager support which the Jews of Palestine above all are already giving. Over 10,000 are now serving with British forces in the Middle East; more than 20,000 are enrolled in various police formations in Palestine and as in this country great numbers are employed in that front line constituted by pursuits and industries essential for the prosecution of war industries and in various services for civil defense.

The first defenses of Palestine are the armies fighting in the western desert in which Palestinians are playing their full part. Our efforts must primarily be concentrated on ensuring success of these armies. His Majesty's Government in the United Kingdom took risks in the dark days in 1942 to discharge their obligations in the Middle East and they have throughout been animated by the determination that the Jewish population in Palestine should in all practicable ways play its part in resistance of the United Nations to oppression and brutalities of Nazi Germany which it is the purpose of your meeting to condemn.

Churchill had seen the situation in Germany for himself. When researching his biography of Marlborough he had visited Munich. While Hitler would not see him, he spoke to Ernst Hanfstaengl, a Harvard alumnus of Roosevelt and a confidant of Hitler, asking: "Why is your chief so violent about the Jews? I can quite understand being angry with the Jews who have done wrong or who are against the country, and I understand resisting them if they try to monopolize power in any walk of life; but what is the sense of being against a man because of his birth? How can a man help how he is born?" Churchill then asked Hanfstaengl to tell Hitler: "Anti-Semitism may be a good starter, but it is a bad finisher."

After things turned against him in Germany, Hanfstaengl escaped to Britain where he was interned as an enemy alien. Then he was sent to the US and worked for the OSS, creating psychological profiles of Hitler and other Nazi leaders.

MADISON SQUARE GARDEN

Madison Square Garden (MSG III, or simply "The Garden") the world famous indoor arena in New York City witnessed many mass rallies and protest meetings from all ends of the political spectrum during the 1930s and 1940s. In 1932 and 1936 Franklin D. Roosevelt made presidential campaign speeches there, and in 1937 the American Jewish Congress sponsored a "Boycott Nazi Germany" protest. In complete contrast a pro-Nazi rally was held at MSG III in 1939 by the subsequently banned German American Bund, an organization consisting only of American citizens of German descent.

In 1941, the America First Committee held an anti-World War II campaign rally, as seen in the photograph, and in 1942, thousands of Jewish citizens and political figures gathered at MSG III to speak out against the atrocities being committed against the Jews in Europe by Hitler's Nazis.

THE FALL OF TOBRUK

That night, Roosevelt and Churchill traveled back to Washington on the Presidential Train, reaching the White House on the morning of June 21. After breakfast, Churchill went to the Oval Office. He was talking with Roosevelt when news came that the Libyan port of Tobruk, where the British had held out under siege for 241 days, had fallen with 35,000 Allied troops taken prisoner.

Erwin Rommel's Afrika Korps was almost at the border of Egypt, which was another devastating blow. The road to Egypt and the oilfields of the Middle East were now opened up. The Soviet Union would then be vulnerable to attack from the south. Meanwhile the Japanese were storming across Asia and there was a very real possibility that Axis forces could take the entire Eurasian landmass.

The shocked silence was broken by Roosevelt asking: "What can we do to help?"

"Give us as many Sherman tanks as you can spare and ship them to the Middle East as quickly as possible," said Churchill.

General Marshall pointed out that the Shermans were only just coming off the production line. The first few hundred had been issued to armored divisions to replace obsolete equipment. Nevertheless, "if the British need is so great, they must have them; and we could let them have a hundred 105mm self-propelling guns in addition," Marshall said. Churchill's chief-of-staff Lieutenant-General Hastings Ismay said:

> *It is interesting to consider what might have happened if that business which they put through in a matter of minutes in the White House had been handled through normal official channels … the chances of this vital equipment arriving in time would have been remote.*

As it was, they arrived in time to play a vital part in the British victory at El Alamein that turned the tide in the war in North Africa.

PUTTING ON A BRAVE FACE

Churchill was crushed by the surrenders at Singapore and Tobruk, but put a brave face on it. Over lunch, Eleanor Roosevelt was amazed by the fortitude of him and her husband.

"To neither of those men was there such a thing as not being able to meet a new

British infantry of the 8th Army at the port of Tobruk, North Africa, during the desert war, 1942.

situation," she said. "I never heard either of them say that ultimately we would not win the war. This attitude was contagious, and no one around either of them would ever have dared to say, 'I'm afraid.'"

Of Roosevelt and Hopkins' reaction to the fall of Tobruk, Churchill said: "Nothing could exceed the sympathy and chivalry of my two friends. There were no reproaches; not an unkind word was spoken." Roosevelt "was very kind."

Privately though, Roosevelt blamed the situation in North Africa partly on Churchill, but mostly on the generals he had picked. He also fretted that soon, the Germans and the Japanese might control everything from the Atlantic in the west to the Pacific in the east.

Churchill then went to South Carolina to see a battalion of American troops make a parachute drop. Churchill was impressed. He also saw a brigade undertake a live-fire exercise, but warned that it took two years to make a soldier.

After boarding the plane home at Baltimore, Churchill learned that his police guard had arrested a lunatic who had come to kill him. When he got home, he faced—and won—a second vote of no confidence. "Good for you," Roosevelt wrote to Churchill from Shangri-la, the presidential retreat later named Camp David by Eisenhower after his grandson.

EL ALAMEIN

The fall of Tobruk had not been quite as catastrophic as Roosevelt and Churchill had feared. The British fell back on a defensive line at El Alamein inside the Egyptian borders and just sixty miles from Alexandria. By the time Rommel reached there, his Afrika Korps was exhausted and its supply lines overextended. Meanwhile a hundred of Roosevelt's self-propelling guns arrived along with three hundred Sherman tanks whose 75mm guns at last gave the British a rival to Rommel's Panzers.

On July 19, 1942, a high level American delegation that included General George Marshall, Admiral Ernest King, and Harry Hopkins arrived at Chequers to discuss "Operation Sledgehammer," the invasion of the Cherbourg Peninsula. Although Churchill also favored "Operation Jupiter," the invasion of Norway, the British proposed "Operation Gymnast," the invasion of French North Africa. The British view prevailed and the Americans agreed to an attack against North Africa, renamed "Operation Torch." On July 27, Roosevelt wrote to Churchill, expressing the view that "the past week represented a turning point in the whole war and that now we are on our way shoulder to shoulder."

Churchill flew to Egypt on August 4 to see what could be done. He gave command of the badly demoralized 8th Army to General Bernard Montgomery and, with the aid of a sandstorm, the British held back the final assault of the Afrika Korps.

HANDLING STALIN WITH CARE

To explain why there would be no second front in Europe that year, Churchill flew on to Moscow after Roosevelt warned him:

Stalin must be handled with great care. We have got always to bear in mind the personality of our ally and the very difficult and dangerous situation that confronts him. No one can be expected to approach the war from a world point of view whose country has been invaded. I think we should try to put ourselves in his place.

Churchill enjoyed himself with Stalin. He explained the situation in North Africa, saying they would be in a position to make a direct attack on France the following year. Churchill said:

To illustrate my point I had meanwhile drawn a picture of a crocodile, and explained to Stalin with the help of this picture how it was our intention to attack the soft belly of the crocodile as we attacked his hard snout. And Stalin, whose interest was now at high pitch, said: "May God prosper this undertaking."

EL ALAMEIN

Before Alamein we never had a victory. After Alamein, we never had a defeat.

Winston Churchill

Fought between October 23 and November 11, 1942, the Battle of El Alamein was the climax and turning point of the North African campaign of World War II. Two famous generals faced each other across the battlefield: General Bernard Montgomery (1887 – 1976) the British commander and Field Marshal Erwin Rommel (1891 – 1944) the German general nicknamed the "Desert Fox."

Rommel's forces were both badly outnumbered and running low on resources, so they constructed a strong defensive position protected by deep minefields. On October 23, following a massive artillery barrage, British infantry and engineers began to pick their way

A German soldier surrenders at El Alamein, North Africa, 1942, signifying the turning point in World War II.

through the deadly minefields. Despite the difficulties and punishing losses, Montgomery held his nerve and after several days of fighting the British achieved a breakthrough on November 4. They captured the bulk of the Axis infantry and began chasing the beaten Afrika Korps back into Libya and Tunisia.

El Alamein was the first decisive victory inflicted by the British Army upon Germany after years of frustration. It was a huge boost to British morale. For Churchill, the victory was a lifeline, restoring British prestige and preventing Roosevelt from reducing Britain to a junior partner in the war. His typical rhetoric at the time helped establish El Alamein as one of the most celebrated victories in British history when he called the battle the "end of the beginning" of World War II.

> Now this is not the end; it is not even the beginning of the end. But it is, perhaps, the end of the beginning.
>
> Winston Churchill

The night before Churchill was leaving he and Stalin had an all-night drinking session, after which even Churchill needed aspirin for breakfast.

Also in August 1942, Roosevelt sent Daniel J. Tobin, president of the Teamsters union, to Britain to investigate labor relations there. He had lunch with Churchill and asked how Roosevelt, Churchill, and Stalin would get along together. Churchill said that he felt Stalin was a man he could work with, though he was not sure that he and Roosevelt could prevent Stalin dominating the post-war world.

Although he had a high opinion of Marshal Stalin, he admired Roosevelt more, again citing his triumph over his physical disability—"the Almighty taking away with one hand the physical strength of a man, but, at the same time, giving with the other a great character that has played such a tremendous part in world affairs in the past few years."

The failure of the Anglo-Canadian raid on the French port of Dieppe, which included fifty US Army Rangers, on August 19, 1942, demonstrated that the Allies were nowhere near ready for a cross-Channel invasion. Roosevelt wrote to Churchill on August 26: "I am concentrating my main thoughts upon Torch from now on, and you may trust me to do my utmost to make your great strategic conception a decisive success."

TOURING WITH THE FIRST LADY

Eleanor Roosevelt visited England in the fall of 1942. "I know our better halves will hit it off beautifully," Roosevelt wrote. He sent Virginia hams that Clementine loved.

In Buckingham Palace with the British royal family, they watched *In Which We Serve*, starring Noël Coward—a movie about the sinking of the destroyer HMS *Kelly*, commanded by Lord Mountbatten, who was present at the screening. Clementine grew worried that Eleanor's exhausting schedule was wearing her out. Churchill tried in vain to take a hand, writing to Roosevelt: "I did my best to advise a reduction of her programme and also interspersing it with blank days, but have not met with success and Mrs. Roosevelt proceeds indefatigably."

While Clementine accompanied Eleanor around—narrowly missing the bombing of Canterbury—she also took the time to write to Roosevelt, saying:

Left-to-right: Winston Churchill, Joseph Stalin, and Averell Harriman, Moscow, 1942.

On each occasion that Winston has been to America he had told me of your great goodness and hospitality to him and I only wish that I could do something adequate to show you how I feel about this. I hope one day to meet you in person and tell you.

Meanwhile Churchill wrote telling him: "Mrs. Roosevelt has been winning golden opinions here from all for her kindness and her unfailing interest in everything we are doing." To the press she talked of a growing understanding between the peoples of the US and the UK, and the prospects of close relations in future.

When Churchill was in the White House he always invited Roosevelt to come over to Great Britain, hopefully in the event of victory or when victory was in sight. Eleanor measured up the doorways of an apartment in Curzon Street, Mayfair, in preparation for a future visit. But there was one issue that she and Churchill argued over—the Spanish Civil War. Churchill told her that, if the Loyalists had won "he and I would have been the first to lose our heads."

OPERATION TORCH

In the first week of September final plans for Operation Torch were hammered out. American troops would land around Casablanca in Morocco and Oran in Algeria, while a joint US-UK force would land around Algiers. When the details were finalized, Roosevelt cabled the one word: "Hurrah!" Churchill replied with the slightly longer: "Okay full blast."

American troops onboard a landing craft heading for the beaches at Oran in Algeria during Operation Torch, November 1942.

At one in the morning on October 24, Churchill cabled Roosevelt, saying:

> *The Battle in Egypt began tonight at eight p.m. London time. The whole force of the Army will be engaged. I will keep you informed. A victory there will be most fruitful to our main enterprise. All the Shermans and self-propelled guns which you gave me on that dark Tobruk morning will play their part.*

By November 6, Churchill was reporting a decisive victory. He cabled:

> *Prisoners estimated now twenty thousand, tanks 350, guns 400, mechanical transports several thousand. Our advanced mobile forces are south of Mersa Matruh [a hundred miles west of El Alamein]. Eighth Army advancing.*

It was indeed a turning point. "Before Alamein we never had a victory," Churchill wrote later. "After Alamein we never had a defeat."

Operation Torch began on November 8 with the landings at Algiers largely unopposed. Those at Oran met stiffer resistance. The landings at Casablanca the following day went ahead without difficulty. On November 10, the fighting ended when the French authorities in Morocco concluded an armistice with the Americans. That day, at the Lord Mayor's Luncheon at the Mansion House in London, Churchill warned: "Now this is not the end. It is not even the beginning of the end. But it is, perhaps, the end of the beginning."

He went on to say: "The British and American affairs continue to prosper in the Mediterranean, and the whole event will be a new bond between the English-speaking peoples and a new hope for the whole world."

BITTER AND BLOODY YEARS

At a picnic at Top Cottage on the last weekend of November, Daisy Suckley sensed that differences would arise between Roosevelt and Churchill over India and the Empire, feeling that Roosevelt would find Stalin easier to deal with. She wrote:

> *He thinks Stalin will understand his plan better than Churchill. In general it consists of an international police force run by the four countries (the United States, Britain, the Soviet Union, and China.) All nations to disarm completely, so that no nation will have the chance to start out to conquer any other. Self determination to be worked out for colonies over a period of years, in the way it was done for the Philippines. I wondered how Empire holders will take to it.*

Roosevelt drove her home, even though he was drunk.

But Churchill had little time for post-war planning. In a broadcast on November 29, he said:

> *I know of nothing that has happened yet which justifies the hope that the war will not be long, or that bitter and bloody years do not lie ahead … Remember that Hitler with his armies and his secret police holds nearly all Europe in his grip. Remember that he has millions of slaves to toil for him, a vast mass of munitions, many mighty arsenals and many fertile fields. Remember that Goering has brazenly declared that whoever starves in Europe it will not be the Germans. Remember that these villains know that their lives are at stake. Remember how small a portion of the German army the British have yet been able to engage and to destroy. Remember that the U-boat warfare is not diminishing but growing, and that it may well be worse before it is better … It may well be that the war in Europe will come to an end before the war in Asia. The Atlantic may be calm, while in the Pacific the hurricane rises to its full pitch. If events should take such a course, we should at once bring all our forces to the other side of the world, to the aid of the United States, to the aid of China, and above all to the aid of our kith and kin in Australia and New Zealand, in their valiant struggle against the aggressions of Japan.*

CHAPTER 12

CASABLANCA

In January 1943, while the Germans were being pushed out of North Africa, Roosevelt and Churchill were to meet in Casablanca. Stalin had been invited but declined. Roosevelt was afraid of flying, particularly long distances over water. It would be the first time any American president had flown. For Churchill it was second nature, even in the dangerous wartime skies.

They met in a complex of villas in the suburb of Anfa, ringing with barbed wire and anti-aircraft guns.

"I think he was delighted to see me," Churchill wrote to Clementine, "and I have a very strong sense of the friendship which prevails between us."

Again they enjoyed late nights together.

Elliott and Franklin Roosevelt Jr. were there, along with Randolph Churchill and Harry Hopkins' son Robert. One night Harry Hopkins rustled up five African-American soldiers who sang for them.

FROM GREEK CLASSICS TO DONALD DUCK

While General Marshall still wanted to make a direct thrust across the English Channel, Churchill wanted to attack what he called the "soft underbelly" of Europe. Roosevelt seemed to hold a position midway between the two. General Dwight D. Eisenhower, commander of Operation Torch, watched Churchill at work:

He was a man of extraordinarily strong convictions and a master in argument and debate. Completely devoted to winning the war and discharging his responsibility as Prime Minister of Great Britain, he was difficult indeed to combat when conviction compelled disagreement with his views. In most cases problems were solved on a basis of almost instant agreement, but intermittently important issues arose where this was far from true. He could become intensely

Roosevelt and Churchill at the Casablanca Conference in Morocco, 1943.

oratorical, even in discussion with a single person, but at the same time his intensity of purpose, made his delivery seem natural and appropriate. He used humor and pathos with equal facility, and drew on everything from the Greek classics to Donald Duck for quotation, cliché, and forceful slang to support his position.

While Churchill won the day at Casablanca—Sicily would be the target—Roosevelt got him to approve the build-up of troops in England, ready for the invasion of France. Roosevelt and Churchill had their meals together and discussed every aspect of the war, from progress on the atomic bomb to who they should recognize as head of the Free French. And they suffered together, dining with the Sultan of Morocco—out of respect for his Muslim faith, it was a dry affair with no alcohol involved.

UNCONDITIONAL SURRENDER

Then on January 24, Roosevelt made the surprise announcement at a press conference that the Allies were demanding "unconditional surrender" from Germany and Japan. Some thought he had made the proposal off the top of his head, but Churchill had in fact already cabled the war cabinet about it. However, Roosevelt liked Churchill's idea of not demanding unconditional surrender from Italy as it might help break up the alliance. The war cabinet did not agree and Roosevelt's final announcement said:

> *The elimination of German, Japanese, and Italian war power means the unconditional surrender by Germany, Italy, and Japan. That means a reasonable assurance of future world peace. It does not mean the destruction of the population of Germany, Italy or Japan, but it does mean the destruction of the philosophies in those countries which are based on conquest and the subjugation of other people.*

THE PARIS OF THE SAHARA

Roosevelt and I drove together the one hundred and fifty miles across the desert—it seemed to me to be beginning to get greener—and reached the famous oasis. My description of Marrakech was—"the Paris of the Sahara," where all the caravans had come from Central Africa for centuries to be heavily taxed en route by the tribes in the mountains and afterwards swindled in the Marrakech markets, receiving the return, which they greatly valued, of the gay life of the city, including fortune-tellers, snake-charmers, masses of food and drink, and on the whole the largest and most elaborately organized brothels in the African continent. All these institutions were of long and ancient repute.

It was agreed between us that I should provide the luncheon, and Tommy was accordingly charged with the task. The President and I drove together all the way, five hours, and talked a great deal of shop, but also touched on lighter matters. Many thousand American troops were posted along the road to protect us from any danger, and aeroplanes circled ceaselessly overhead.

From Winston Churchill's account of the journey to Marrakech.

THE SNOWS OF THE ATLAS MOUNTAINS

When the conference was over, Churchill said to Roosevelt: "You cannot come all this way to North Africa without seeing Marrakech. Let us spend two days there. I must be with you when you see the sunset on the snows of the Atlas Mountains."

They took an olive-drab Daimler limousine across the desert the next day. Others went along for the ride. Averell Harriman recalled in his memoirs:

> *As soon as the press conference was over, the two were off to Marrakech with Hopkins and Harriman [referring to himself in the*

third person], the Prime Minister's son Randolph, Hopkins' son Robert, Admiral [Ross T.] McIntire [Roosevelt's personal physician] and an entourage of aides. It was a four-hour drive of 150 miles through the desert, the dusty road lined with American soldiers standing at attention while fighter planes swept overhead. The British had prepared a picnic lunch of hard-boiled eggs, sandwiches and mince pies to eat along the way.

According to Hopkins, there was more than just a picnic lunch. As the British had fixed up the lunch there was also plenty of wine and Scotch.

DANCERS AND SNAKE CHARMERS

Arriving in Marrakech that evening, they stayed in a plush villa called La Saadia which had been left in the care of the US vice consul Kenneth Pendar by an American heiress, an arch-Republican. When she learned that FDR had stayed there, she vowed never to visit the house again.

According to Hopkins, Pendar was an archaeologist who had been an American secret agent in North Africa before the landings. Pendar recalled:

Both Mr. Roosevelt and Mr. Churchill were in high spirits, and spoke with admiration of the superb view of the Atlas Mountains they had seen for the last fifty miles or so of their journey. This was the President's first trip to Morocco, but the Prime Minister had been in Marrakech before, and had even gone up into the Atlas to the casbah of the Galoui at Telouet. As we drank our tea, Robert Hopkins, Harry Hopkins' son, made a film of the occasion.

The younger members of the party went off to explore the town, Hopkins wrote:

Averell [Harriman], Randolph [Churchill], Robert [Hopkins, Harry's son] and I went to visit a big fair—storytellers—dancers—snake-charmers—and 15,000 natives. Very colorful. The great trading market was near—but nothing much to sell—tho thousands ever milling thru.

Franklin Roosevelt and Winston Churchill in Marrakech, Morocco, 1943. Roosevelt sits in a wicker chair so he can comfortably enjoy the view.

The villa was equipped with a tower. After tea, Churchill asked Pendar to show him up to the top of the tower.

"As we climbed up, I saw his shrewd eyes taking everything in," said Pendar. "From the open terrace he told me how much he loved Marrakech and how much he had enjoyed sketching here before the war, during his last visit."

He asked Pendar whether it would be possible to arrange for Roosevelt to be brought up there.

"I am so fond of this superb view that it has been my dream to see it with him," said Churchill. "All during the conference I have looked forward to coming down here to this beautiful spot."

AIN'T NO WAR

On the way back down the tower, Churchill counted the steps. There were sixty of them. Churchill then went to get Roosevelt.

"Mr. President," he said. "Both Mr. Pendar and I are most anxious for you to see the view from the tower. Do you think you could be persuaded to make the trip?"

Roosevelt said he had every intention of going up the tower if someone would carry him. Two aides carried Roosevelt up the stairs with his legs "dangling like the limbs of a ventriloquist's dummy," according to Churchill's doctor. Another aide went ahead to open doors. Churchill suggested they bring a wicker chair in case the President wanted to rest along the way. Then he brought up the rear, humming and singing: "Oh, there ain't no war, there ain't no war." Roosevelt laughed.

A chair was arranged on the parapet that commanded the entire view of the High Atlas range. Roosevelt and Churchill watched as the sun set over the mountains. The vice consul described the scene:

We all looked out for a quarter of an hour or so at this most superb view. Never have I seen the sun set on those snow-capped peaks with such magnificence. There had evidently been snow storms recently in the mountains,

for they were white almost to their base, and looked more wild and rugged than ever, their sheer walls rising some 12,000 feet before us. The range runs more or less from east to west, and the setting sun over the palm oasis to our right shed a pink light on the snowy flank of the mountains. With the clear air, and the snow on the range, it looked near enough for us to reach out and touch its magnificence.

"It's the most lovely spot in the world," Churchill said to Roosevelt. It grew cold and Churchill sent for Roosevelt's coat, which he draped around the president's shoulders.

"Just as the sun set (we were all silent) the electric light on the top of every mosque tower in Marrakech flashed on to indicate to the faithful the hour of prayer," Pendar wrote. "Both Mr. Roosevelt and Mr. Churchill were spellbound by the view, but it became perceptibly colder, and the whole party started down again."

"The great men went to their rooms to rest and dress before dinner," wrote Pendar, "while the younger fry had drinks."

SONGS AND TOASTS

Cocktails were at eight. For dinner, Churchill donned a siren suit and monogrammed black velvet slippers, while Roosevelt reclined on a couch, sipping an old fashioned.

"I am the Pasha," he told Pendar. "You may kiss my hand."

"We had a very jolly dinner, about fifteen or sixteen," said Churchill, "and we all sang songs. I sang, and the President joined in the choruses, and at one moment was about to try a solo. However, someone interrupted and I never heard this."

Pendar sat at the head of the table, seating Roosevelt on his right and Churchill on his left. Harriman sat beside Roosevelt, and Hopkins next to Churchill. Pendar's servant Louis served lobster, filet mignon, and salad with paté. This was followed by a huge mound of profiteroles around three feet high.

"I see the pastry cooks have been busy for days and days, preparing for our secret visit," said Churchill. He looked disconcerted and said: "How on earth does one attack a thing like that?"

He looked up at the soldier proffering it and said: "My man, you should pass that to the President first."

The soldier did as he was told and stepped round to Roosevelt, who said: "Why that's easy, Winston, this is the way you do it." And he simply took off the top of the tower of profiteroles and put it on his plate. Harriman recalled the scene:

> *There were speeches, songs and toasts. It was the President's habit to shift gears conversationally when he preferred not to discuss weighty matters. This time he expounded to Pendar and Harriman his views about independence for Morocco*

on the Philippine pattern. He talked of compulsory education, of fighting disease through immunization and of birth control. Occasionally, the P.M. interjected a pessimistic—and realistic—note. He doesn't like the new ideas but accepts them as inevitable.

ECLIPSING CHURCHILL

Pendar raised the subject of General Charles de Gaulle, the candidate he favored as head of the Free French.

"Oh, let's don't speak of him," said Churchill. "We call him Jeanne d'Arc and we're looking for some bishops to burn him." Then Roosevelt and Churchill had their usual spat over India, Harriman recalled:

Roosevelt and Churchill announcing at a press conference that the Allies will be demanding an unconditional surrender from Germany, Italy, and Japan, Casablanca, January 1943.

THE GREATEST TWO MEN OF THE AGE

The Prime Minister made no secret of his determination to preserve the British Empire, although he knew that would be difficult. Roosevelt enjoyed thinking aloud on the tremendous changes he saw ahead—the end of colonial empires and the rise of newly independent nations across the sweep of Africa and Asia … He recognized the rise of nationalism among the colonial peoples. He also recognized that Churchill was pretty much a nineteenth-century colonialist. So he said some of these things partly to jar Churchill but also from a fundamental belief that the old order could not last. All this was surely in Churchill's mind when he later said that he had not become Prime Minister to preside over the liquidation of the British Empire.

Throughout this, their final evening together, Churchill kept looking for an opportunity to talk privately with Roosevelt. Harriman thought that Churchill wanted to address the question of "unconditional surrender" once more. But the seating arrangement, to Churchill's great annoyance, made a *tête-à-tête* impossible.

"Roosevelt rather liked the idea," Harriman recalled, "that he did not have to go through with this talk. He always enjoyed other people's discomfort. I think it is fair to say that it never bothered him very much when other people were unhappy." In his account of the evening, Pendar noted:

I was struck by the fact that, though Mr. Churchill spoke much more amusingly than the President, it was Mr. Roosevelt who dominated any room they were in, not merely because he was President of the United States, but because he had more spiritual quality than Mr. Churchill, and, I could not help but feel, a more profound understanding of human beings. I was very much surprised by this because, having seen Mr. Churchill often in the pre-war days, I had felt sure that no one could eclipse his personality.

AFTER MIDNIGHT

After midnight, they moved into the salon where a table was laid out with drinks, sandwiches, and other snacks. There they worked on what they were going to tell Stalin about the decisions they had made at Casablanca. They knew that he would not be pleased and he was already complaining that he was doing most of the fighting against the Nazis. They also had to send a summary to Generalissimo Chiang Kai-shek, the Chinese leader. "After a nibble or two the two great men set to work," said Pendar.

Work continued until 3:30 a.m. when the documents were completed and in their

THE SALON AT LA SAADIA

The problem was to arrange a temporary sort of writing table for them and adequate light; the salon at La Saadia was not meant for work. We finally perched a lamp up high on two tables, so as to give adequate light, and arranged two chairs on either side. Then Mr. Hopkins and Mr. Harriman sat down to work with them. They were composing a summary of the Anfa Conference and messages to General Chiang Kai-shek and Marshal Stalin. The Prime Minister's two secretaries, Mr. Rowan and Mr. Martin, were established in the library, typing and drafting

these documents. Mr. Hopkins and Mr. Harriman would take parts of them to their separate rooms and work on them and then come back to the salon and show them to the Big Two. The rest of us went outside into the courtyard, and some of the party went to bed. From time to time, work would stop for a moment, and we would all be called in for a drink or a sandwich, and a joke or two. At one point the President was wheeled into his room so that he could work alone at a dressing-table which he used as a desk.

Kenneth Pendar, *Adventure in Diplomacy*

final order. Roosevelt and Churchill seemed relieved and pleased, Pendar recalled:

> *Both men had a catching quality of optimism, but with the President I kept feeling that it was tinged with a deep realization of far distant and overall problems. The Prime Minister seemed much more in the present and more of an extrovert. The President, on the other hand, often sat gazing into space as he worked. That night he had a look that was not exactly sad, yet it was the look of someone who comprehended sadness.*

Roosevelt was due to leave at 7:30 a.m. the next day. Over a nightcap, he said to Churchill: "Now, Winston, don't you get up in the morning to see me off. I'll be wheeled into your room to kiss you goodbye."

But Churchill would not hear of it.

"Not at all, Mr. President," he said. "I can get into my rompers in two ticks, and I will be on hand to see you off." As Churchill recalled it:

> *My illustrious colleague was to depart just after dawn on the 25th for his long flight by Lagos and Dakar and so across to Brazil and then up to Washington. We had parted the night before, but he came round in the morning on the way to the aeroplane to say another good-bye. I was in bed, but would not hear of letting him go to the airfield alone, so I jumped up and put on my zip [siren suit], and nothing else except slippers, and in this informal garb I drove with him to the airfield, and went on the plane and saw him comfortably settled down, greatly admiring his courage under all his physical disabilities and feeling very anxious about the hazards he had to undertake. These aeroplane journeys had to be taken as a matter of course during the war. None the less I always regarded them as dangerous excursions.*

THE HARD ROAD AHEAD

Pendar recalled it rather differently. He said Churchill appeared in the weirdest outfit he had ever seen—rompers, velvet slippers, an air marshal's blue cap, and a flowing dressing gown with a red dragon on it and a black velvet collar and cuffs, made out of what looked like patchwork quilt. Hopkins, who was leaving too, said: "Churchill had suddenly decided to drive out to the field with us, wearing his ever flaming bathrobe, bedroom slippers and the inevitable cigar. Churchill and I took one last walk together—he is pleased by the conference—expressed great confidence of victory—but warned of the hard road ahead."

Churchill ran up the wooden ramps into the airplane to see where Roosevelt was going to sit. On his way back down the ramp, photographers stepped forward and started taking pictures of the Prime Minister in his very original costume. Churchill stopped, pulled the cigar out of his mouth and, using it as a pointer, shook it at them with a smile and said: "You simply cannot do this to me." They laughed and lowered their cameras.

As the plane prepared to leave, Churchill turned to his doctor Charles Wilson and said: "I love these Americans. They have behaved so generously."

Churchill then grabbed the US vice consul's arm and said: "Come, Pendar, let's go home. I don't like to see them take off."

THE TRUEST FRIEND AND THE GREATEST MAN

From the car, Pendar looked back to see the plane start up and the engines roared. "Don't tell me when they take off," said Churchill, grabbing Pendar's arm again. "It makes me far too nervous. If anything happened to that man, I couldn't stand it. He is the truest friend; he has the farthest vision; he is the greatest man I have ever known." After a period of silence, Churchill asked Pendar:

> *Don't you think your countrymen will be thrilled when they hear that their President has flown here with the courage of an eagle, and has seen and reviewed the troops in the theater of battle? Don't you think they will be universally thrilled by this, and that it will catch their imagination?*

Churchill returned to work in the villa for another two days, but took time out to paint the vista Roosevelt has seen from the top of the tower. It was the only painting he attempted during the war. He later gave it to Roosevelt. When he died, it passed to Eleanor, who gave it to Elliott. He sold it and it ended up in the hands of a private collector.

THE WORLD'S WORST PATIENT

After Casablanca, both men fell ill. Churchill came down with pneumonia, while Roosevelt suffered a slight fever after his stop in The Gambia, though he was happy to exaggerate the symptoms, telling Churchill:

I think I picked up sleeping sickness or Gambia fever or some kindred bug in that hell-hole of yours called Bathurst [now Banul, the capital]. It laid me low—four days in bed—then a lot of sulfathiazole [an antibiotic] which cured the fever and left me feeling like a wet rag. I was no good after 2 p.m. and, after standing it for a week or so, I went to Hyde Park for five days; got full health in glorious zero weather—came back here last week and have been feeling like a fighting cock ever since.

He was also concerned for Churchill's health, saying: "Please, please, for the sake of the world, don't overdo these days. You must remember that it takes about a month of occasional let-

A desert palm grove in Marrakech with the dramatic snow-capped Atlas mountains behind.

ups to get back your full strength ... Tell Mrs. Churchill that when I was laid up I was a thoroughly model patient and that I hope you will live down the reputation in our press of having been the 'world's worst patient.'"

January 30, 1943, was Roosevelt's sixty-first birthday. Churchill wrote: "Many happy and glorious returns of the day from your friend. Winston."

The New York Times also celebrated the occasion, saying:

Gone are the days when the democracies shivered in their boots while two scrubby dictators put their heads together at the top of the Brenner Pass. It is for the dictators to speculate and shiver now.

We do not underrate the stubborn genius of Winston Churchill when we say that this shift of the strategic climate has been brought about by Franklin D. Roosevelt. It would be an undemocratic folly to pretend that no other American could have led us successfully in this war. It just happens that he is leading us, that he has found the words to express what we all feel, that he has inspired deeds of which we are all proud.

On that same day, the German command post at Stalingrad had been overrun by the Soviet Union after a six-month siege. Two entire German armies were wiped out including their reserves. Some 330,000 of Germany's finest troops were killed.

Churchill's painting of the sunset over the Atlas mountains.

CHAPTER 13

FORWARD INTO BATTLE

On May 11, 1943, Churchill arrived at the White House again after crossing the Atlantic on the *Queen Mary*, along with five thousand German prisoners of war. Eleanor Roosevelt was given just a few hours warning of his arrival. Four days earlier, Tunis had fallen to the British and the whole of North Africa was in Allied hands. Churchill was in ebullient mood, reciting limericks and telling risqué stories about Belgian "tarts." They watched the unreleased movie *The Battle of Britain* and Churchill wept.

During the Trident strategy talks Roosevelt and Churchill again discussed the second front that Stalin was pushing for. George Marshall once more demanded an attack across the English Channel, while Churchill argued for his "soft underbelly" strategy. According to the duty officer in the White House Map Room during the discussions: "The President sat back and listened very carefully; Churchill never sat back. Roosevelt would let the others duke it out, but not Churchill."

He noted: "Americans overwhelmed by British oratory." Nevertheless a date was set for a cross-Channel invasion—May 1, 1944. The Americans made a joke of Churchill's reluctance, saying that Stalin would be in Calais before the Allies were. To those on the inside, it was clear that, while Churchill was the towering figure who had kept Hitler at bay, he was soon going to be overshadowed by Roosevelt.

FDR with Winston Churchill, together again in Washington, for the Trident strategy talks, 1943.

SPARE YOUR COUNTRY'S FLAG

Roosevelt and Churchill drove up to Shangri-La for the weekend with Eleanor and Hopkins. There was a disagreement in the White House driveway when Mrs. Roosevelt proposed sitting in the jump seat so Churchill could sit next to the President.

"I would not have this, and the British Empire went into action," said Churchill. "After about three minutes conflict of wills, I won, and Mrs. Roosevelt took her proper place by her husband's side."

Passing through the town of Frederick, Maryland, Churchill asked about a roadside sign in the shape of a giant peppermint stick advertising Barbara Frietchie candy, named after a character from the Civil War whom John Greenleaf Whittier wrote a famous poem about. Roosevelt recited the only two lines of the poem that he and most other people can remember:

"Shoot, if you must, this old gray head,
But spare your country's flag," she said.

Churchill went on to recite all thirty rhyming couplets, though he claimed not to have looked at the poem in thirty years. "I got full marks from my highly select American audience, none of whom corrected my many misquotations," he said.

THE ROAD TO GETTYSBURG

Along the way, Churchill saw the sign for Gettysburg, which was just forty miles away. "Why, this may have been the very road by which Longstreet moved up," said Churchill, "and I was encouraged to discuss at some length the characters of Stonewall Jackson and Robert E. Lee, two of the noblest men ever born on the American continent."

Roosevelt and Churchill were both interested in military history and frequently discussed it. But on this occasion Churchill's

ANGLO-AMERICAN SUPERIORITY

On May 22, 1943, Vice President Henry A. Wallace had lunch with the President and Churchill, who held forth. Wallace recorded it in his diary:

He made it more clear than he had at the luncheon on Saturday that he expected England and the United States to run the world and he expected the staff organizations which had been set up for winning the war to continue when the peace came, that these staff organizations would by mutual understanding really run the world even though there was a supreme council and three regional councils.

I said bluntly that I thought the notion of Anglo-Saxon superiority, inherent in Churchill's approach, would be offensive to many of the nations of the world as well as to a number of people in the United States. Churchill had had quite a bit of whiskey, which, however, did not affect the clarity of his thinking process but did perhaps increase his frankness. He said why be apologetic about Anglo-Saxon superiority, that we were superior, that we

had the common heritage which had been worked out over the centuries in England and had been perfected by our constitution. He himself was half American, he felt that he was called on as a result to serve the function of uniting the two great Anglo-Saxon civilizations in order to confer the benefit of freedom on the rest of the world.

I suggested it might be a good plan to bring in the Latin American nations so that the citizens of the New World and the British Empire could all travel freely without passports. Churchill did not like this. He said that if we took all the colors on the painter's palette and mix them up together, we get just a smudgy gray brown. I interjected, "And so you believe in the pure Anglo-Saxon race. Anglo-Saxondom über alles?" He said his concept was not a race concept but a concept of common ideals and common history.

oration seems to have been a monologue. "After a while," he noted, "silence and slumber descended upon the company, as we climbed with many a twist and turn up the spurs of the Alleghenies."

In his memoirs, Churchill said of Shangri-La: "It is principally a log cabin, with all modern improvements. In front is a fountain and a pool of clear water, in which swam a number of large trout, newly caught in a neighboring stream, and awaiting the consummation of their existence."

For perhaps half an hour Churchill watched as Roosevelt stuck stamps into his album "and so forgot the cares of state." But not for long as Churchill recalled:

Soon another car drove up to the door, and out stepped General Bedell Smith, quick-winged from Eisenhower's headquarters, with a budget of serious questions on which decisions were urgently required. So sadly FDR left his stamp collection and addressed himself to his task … By evening we were all tired out, and went to bed at ten.

The two world leaders did get to spend some time relaxing over drinks and smoking on the veranda of the Bear's Den, the name Roosevelt gave the Aspen Lodge. Churchill went to the Cozy Restaurant in nearby Thurmont, where he enjoyed a cold beer and gave a waitress some coins for the jukebox.

Franklin Roosevelt and Winston Churchill fishing at Shangri-La, Maryland, May 1943.

FISHING AT SHANGRI-LA

They were also taken by backroads to Hunting Creek, a mountain stream that crossed the road to Shangri-La about two miles west of the entrance. A six-mile stretch of the creek between its source near Foxville and the Thurmont municipal dam had been heavily stocked with brook trout and set aside for fly fishing, although most local fishermen used bait. The fishing spot chosen by FDR and his guest was an old ore pit of the Catoctin Iron Furnace, a Thurmont industry in pre-revolutionary days. With an aide and a secret service man within earshot, the President and Prime Minister sat on the bank in portable canvas chairs.

Later Roosevelt sent photographs of the fishing trip to Churchill. The pictures, taken in the shade of the hickories along Hunting Creek, were dark. Roosevelt apologized that they "did not turn out very well but at least it proves that you and I tried to catch a fish. Better luck next time."

However, all was not peace and harmony at Shangri-La. Roosevelt invited Lord Beaverbrook to stay as well. Beaverbrook tried to wriggle out of it, knowing that his presence would not be welcomed by Churchill. But Hopkins phoned him and informed him that the President of the United States was not in the habit of having his invitations turned down. Beaverbrook was forced to comply. He recalled the scene:

> Roosevelt sat in a big chair, his wheelchair placed in a corner between two windows so that he got the bright light. Churchill, at his side, was pressing for tanks, oil, and every conceivable article of war. And Roosevelt was dodging all the while—he would have to consult George Marshall, he said, or one or another person. Roosevelt would bring their conversations to an end by taking out his stamp book. "Isn't this a beauty from Newfoundland?" he would say. And Churchill would stump off into another room, fretting at the delay.

WINSTON HOURS

On other occasions, to relieve Roosevelt from "Winston hours," an aide would summon the President to an imaginary phone call. At some point during the weekend, the conversation turned to the second front and Beaverbrook argued for the invasion of western France rather than Italy. Churchill erupted, telling him that he had no business involving himself in strategy and accusing him of being disloyal to his country. Beaverbrook stormed out in anger and returned to Washington. For the next month, he continued to undermine Churchill by lobbying Hopkins and others for a cross-Channel invasion rather than an attack on Italy.

But generally, the weekend at Shangri-La was a success. "My friendship with the President was vastly stimulated," Churchill wrote to Clementine. "We could not have been on easier terms."

Another guest, Roosevelt's daughter Anna, remembered:

> It was a beautiful spot and dinner was fun. This evening I also discovered for the first time that the P.M. picks his teeth all through dinner and uses snuff liberally. The sneezes which follow the latter practically rock the foundations of the house and he then blows his nose about three times like a foghorn. I admired his snuff box and found it was one that had once belonged to Lord Nelson—and then, like the idiot I am, I allowed him to badger me into trying some of the snuff. No sneezes came to relieve the tickle in my snozzle and I wept copious tears for at least five minutes! The P.M. teased me unmercifully for not taking enough.

MEETING UNCLE JOE

However, while all this conviviality was taking place, Roosevelt was going behind Churchill's back. He had sent former Ambassador Joseph E. Davies to Moscow carrying a private letter asking to see Stalin, or "Uncle Joe" as they called him, without Churchill and without telling him.

"Three is a crowd and we can arrange for the Big Three to get together thereafter," Roosevelt told Davies. "Churchill will understand. I will take care of that."

Harriman told Churchill about the letter after he got back to London. On June 25, Churchill cabled Roosevelt saying:

> Averell told me last night of your wish for a meeting with U.J. in Alaska. The whole world is expecting and all our side are desiring a meeting of the three great powers at which, not only the political chiefs, but the military staffs would be present in order to plan the future war moves and, of course, search for the foundations of post-war settlement. It would be a pity to draw U.J. 7000 miles from Moscow for anything less than this …

He suggested they meet in Scapa Flow, in the Orkney Islands, Scotland.

> … You must excuse me expressing myself with all the frankness that our friendship and the gravity of the issue warrant. I do not

underrate the use that enemy propaganda would make of a meeting between the heads of Soviet Russia and the United States at this juncture with the British Commonwealth and Empire excluded. It would be serious and vexatious, and many would be bewildered and alarmed thereby. My journey to Moscow with Averell in August 1942 was on altogether a lower level, and at a stage in the war when we had only to explain why no second front. Nevertheless, whatever you decide, I shall sustain to the best of my ability here.

TELLING AN OUTRIGHT LIE

Roosevelt's reply was an outright lie: "I did not suggest to UJ that we meet alone but he told Davies that he assumed (a) that we would meet alone and (b) that he agreed that we should not bring staffs to what would be a preliminary meeting."

He went on to suggest that Stalin might be "more frank" if they met alone: "What would you think of coming over soon afterwards and that you and I with staffs should meet in the Citadel in Quebec?" he said. "It is far better than Washington at that time of year … While UJ gave no definite dates he suggested the end of July or early August." He went on:

> Of course, you and I are completely frank in matters of this kind and I agree with you that later in the autumn we should most definitely have a full dress meeting with the Russians. That is why I think of a visit with Stalin as a preparatory talk on what you rightly call a lower level. Finally I gather from Davies the Kremlin people do not at all like the idea of UJ flying across Finland, Sweden, Norway, and the North Sea to Scapa, especially at this time of year when there is practically no darkness.

In the event, Stalin put an end to Roosevelt's plans for a meeting when he realized that Roosevelt and Churchill had postponed any cross-Channel attack from 1943 to May 1, 1944.

Ambassador Joseph E. Davies.

SHOULDER TO SHOULDER

Churchill addressed the US Congress again on May 19. He began by saying:

> For over five hundred days we have toiled, suffered and dared, shoulder to shoulder, against a cruel and mighty enemy. We have acted in close combination and concert in many parts of the world—on land and sea, and in the air. The fact that you have invited me to come to Congress for the second time is certainly a high mark in my life. It also shows that our partnership has not done so badly. I am proud that you have found us good Allies, striving forward in comradeship to the accomplishment of our task without grudging, stinting either life, treasure, or, indeed, anything we have to give.

He was applauded when he promised that "the British will fight alongside America against Japan while breath remains in our bodies and blood flows in our veins." He then looked back on the fall of Tobruk and how Roosevelt had come to the rescue:

> It was indeed a dark, bitter hour for me. I will never forget the kindness and delicacy of the true comradeship of our American friends in adversity. Their only thought was to find means of helping to restore the situation. Never did they question the resolution or fighting quality of our troops. Hundreds of Sherman tanks taken from an American division were sent with the utmost speed around the Cape of Good Hope to Egypt. When one ship carrying fifty tanks was torpedoed the United States replaced it and its precious vehicles before we even thought of asking them to do so. The Sherman tank was the best tank in the desert in 1942 and played a more appreciable part in the ruin of Rommel's army at Alamein and the subsequent pursuit.

CHURCHILL'S GREATEST FEAR

Many congressmen said this speech was the greatest of Churchill's career. Senator Lucas Scott of Illinois said it was a complete answer to those who wanted to plan war strategy on the floor of the Senate. He went to have secret discussions with the Foreign Relations Committees of the Senate and House of Representatives.

During their chats in the White House, the subject of the 1944 presidential election came up. Churchill told Roosevelt: "I simply can't go on without you." Roosevelt leaving the White House was Churchill's greatest fear. He wrote to Clementine, saying:

> Although after twelve arduous years he would gladly be quit of it, it would be painful to leave with the war unfinished and break the theme of his action. To me this would be a disaster of the first magnitude. There is no one to replace him, and all my hopes for the Anglo-American future would be withered for the lifetime of the present generation—probably for the present century.

Winston Churchill addresses a special joint session of Congress, May 19, 1943.

THE JEWISH REFUGEE PROBLEM

While Churchill was in Washington, he and Roosevelt discussed what they should do about Jewish refugees. Again on June 30, Churchill cabled:

> *The need for assistance to refugees, in particular Jewish refugees, has not grown less since we discussed the question, and all possible outlets need to be kept open. Of these the most practical still is North Africa, and I hope that the difficulties over the proposed refugee camp there have now been cleared up, and that an early practical decision is now possible. Our immediate facilities for helping the victims of Hitler's Anti-Jewish drive are so limited at present that the opening of the small camp proposed for the purpose of removing some of them to safety seems all the more incumbent on us, and I should be grateful if you could let me know whether it has been found possible to bring the scheme into operation.*

Roosevelt agreed, but with the Nazi's "Final Solution" now in operation, few were rescued.

A BATTLE OF IDEAS

Things did not always go smoothly between Roosevelt and Churchill. Learning that Roosevelt had told his cabinet that if Churchill had one hundred ideas a day, four of them might be good, Churchill responded: "It [was] impertinent for Roosevelt to say this. It comes badly from a man who hadn't had any ideas at all."

On the other hand Churchill complained of Roosevelt's tendency to "follow public opinion rather than to form it and lead it."

However, Roosevelt sometimes also found Churchill's persistence tiresome. He told Roald Dahl, fighter pilot, British secret service agent, and later renowned children's author, who was visiting Washington: "I have had four dispatches from Winston today, one only a few minutes ago, and I have replied to each one of them. That is equivalent to writing four full pages of newspaper articles."

Later, over drinks, Dahl asked Roosevelt what he would think of Churchill as a post-war premier. "Well, I don't know," said Roosevelt. "I think I would give him two years after the war has finished."

Jewish refugees fleeing Germany.

POST-WAR PROSPECTS

Of his own post-war prospects Roosevelt said the American people "have seen so much of me and had me for so long that they will now do anything for a change. They're restless because they have nothing against me, but they have, as I said, seen so much of me that they want someone else. They just want a change. But mark my words, after two years they will be shouting and yelling to get back to what they had before."

Though the Roosevelt-Stalin meeting was off, the meeting in Quebec was still going ahead. This time Churchill, now code named "Warden," would be accompanied by "Mrs. Warden"—Clementine—and "Lt. Mary Warden"—Mary Churchill. But Clementine was exhausted and stayed behind in Quebec while Churchill and Mary traveled on to Hyde Park. Eleanor was planning a secret trip to the Pacific. Later she wrote in her column:

> *Prime Minister Churchill, who was staying with us, still speaks occasionally of how surprised he was when I casually mentioned at dinner one night that I was leaving the next day for the Southwest Pacific. He looked aghast … Mr. Churchill insisted on cabling to all his people in the Pacific and they were most kind wherever I met them.*

PICNIC WITH THE PRESIDENT

They visited Eleanor's cottage Val-Kill for a picnic. She set up two card tables carrying everything they needed for a large picnic lunch, alongside a broiler on wheels to cook hotdogs. For the occasion, Churchill wore a "ten gallon" Stetson, sipped on Scotch kept cool in an ice pail, and ate one and a half hotdogs, giving the other half to Fala, the President's black Scottish Terrier. Daisy Suckley, who had given the dog to the President, was there too, and observed Churchill closely.

> *He is a strange looking little man. Fat and round, his clothes bunched up on him. Practically no hair on his head. He talks as though he had terrible adenoids—sometimes*

> *says very little, then talks quite a lot—His humorous twinkle is infectious. Mary and he are evidently very close; now and then they would joke together.*

Then they went swimming, Daisy said:

> *Mrs. R. came & made a dive and a splash or two. The PM decided to go in, too. In a pair of shorts, he looked exactly like a kewpie. He made a good dive in, soon came out, wrapped a large wool blanket around himself and sat down to talk to F.D.R.*

Daisy Suckley also recorded her general impression of the company:

> *I took away the impression that Ch. adores the P., loves him, as a man, looks up to him, defers to him, leans on him. He is older than the P., but the P. is the bigger person, and Churchill recognizes it. I saw in Churchill, too, an amount of real greatness I did not suspect before. Speaking of South Africa, Ch. said General [and Prime Minister Jan] Smuts is one of the really great men of the world—"a prophet— a seer"— his very words—He wants to get him to London, for his "mind on post war Europe" … The P. was relaxed and seemingly cheerful in the midst of the deepest problems. Mrs. R. is taking a flying trip of six weeks to the South Pacific. The P. wants me to go to Washington to help take care of Mrs. Churchill when the three come down about the 26th.*

LESS THAN IMPRESSED

Serious talks also went on that weekend. They decided who should command the cross-Channel invasion, now code named Overlord, and would invite Stalin to meet with the two of them in Alaska that fall. The atomic bomb was another topic of conversation. They drew up an agreement to share the results of the Manhattan Project, keep it secret, and not to use the weapon against each other, or anyone else without mutual consent. The memo was signed by the two men.

Roosevelt traveled up to Quebec on the train with Churchill. When Clementine Churchill met Roosevelt she was less than impressed, particularly because he had the cheek to call her "Clemmie."

"She respected him enormously, but she was also a sharp spotter of clay feet," said Mary Churchill. "She found him very vain."

Queen Victoria's granddaughter, Princess Alice, was the wife of the Earl of Athlone, Canada's governor-general. She wanted Roosevelt and Churchill to sign her autograph book. George Elsey remembered taking it to Roosevelt to sign:

> *I took it, and it had everybody in it you could think of: the Kaiser, the Czar, countless royal names that didn't mean anything to me. When the President came in, I handed the Princess's collection to him, and Roosevelt sat there in wonder. As he took my Waterman in hand to sign, he said, "How my mother would have loved this."*

Churchill was less star-struck and signed the autograph book without a second thought.

FICTITIOUS PHONE CALLS

When the Quebec conference got down to business, Roosevelt's naval aide Admiral Wilson Brown noted: "There was always a good deal of chaffing between the two leaders. Both seemed to enjoy the give and take of friendly sparring to reach a compromise."

But there was much they could be pleased with. By the time they reached Quebec, Brown said, "We had driven the Germans out of Africa and Sicily; we had landed in Italy, and Mussolini's fall was expected at any moment." When it came to the cross-Channel attack, Brown recalled:

> *The Prime Minister's lively imagination was working at full blast. The problems facing the conference were for the Normandy landing—how much steel could be spared to build landing craft, landing piers and temporary harbors without interfering with the shipbuilding schedule already underway to maintain our steady flow of troops to England with necessary supplies and equipment.*

Quebec Conference, August 1943. Left to right: MacKenzie King, the Earl of Athlone, Franklin D. Roosevelt, Princess Alice, and Winston Churchill.

Churchill and Roosevelt were so absorbed by the details, so "excited and enthusiastic," that Brown had to intervene to limit the "Winston hours" from exhausting Roosevelt.

"To break up a night session I several times invented a fictitious telephone call from Washington when I could tell by [Roosevelt's] expression that he had had enough," said Brown. "He was always pleased by the subterfuge."

But things at the conference were not always so serious. After taking a sip of iced water, Churchill remarked: "This water tastes funny."

"Of course it does," said Harry Hopkins. "It's got no whisky in it."

On August 15, 1943, some 35,000 US and Canadian troops landed on Kiska Island in the Aleutians, which had been occupied by the Japanese the previous year. But the Japanese had evacuated the island on July 28 and all the Allied Force found were barking dogs. Every time Churchill entered the map room, he would say: "How are we today—woof, woof, woof."

It was funny the first time, but then began to grate and it annoyed Roosevelt enormously.

FULL OF BRIGHT IDEAS

The two men were united again in the face of a stiff cable from Stalin, rebuking them for not involving him in the negotiations over the surrender of Italy signed on September 3. They took a little time out to go fishing. Churchill caught one fish, while Roosevelt caught none at all, so he named the fishing hole "One Lake"—ignoring the fact that the rest of the party had caught plenty.

The joke persisted when Churchill took a sojourn in the mountains after the conference. "I hope Lady Warden is getting a real rest and that you are also," wrote Roosevelt who was at Hyde Park, taking a break from his occasionally tiresome companion. "Also hope you have gone to One Lake. Be sure to have the big ones weighed and verified by Mackenzie King."

Churchill stayed in a log cabin where he relaxed in hot baths and sat round a log fire in the evening singing songs by his friend Noël Coward and favorites by Dan Leno and the previous generation of music-hall stars. He had a cold when he arrived at the White House on September 1, while Roosevelt also looked tired and had dark rings under his eyes.

American soldiers building fires and cooking near wrecked Japanese equipment on the island of Kiska, during the Aleutian Islands campaign.

Nevertheless, Churchill still kept the President up talking until 2 a.m.

The late nights were taking their toll on Roosevelt. "I'm nearly dead," he told Labor Secretary Frances Perkins. "I have to talk to the PM all night, and he gets bright ideas in the middle of the night and comes pattering down the hall to my bedroom in his bare feet … I have to have my sleep."

He complained that he got so sleepy that his brain would not work, so he decided to take a nap. But before he could nod off, in breezed Churchill full of clever schemes.

MARRIED TO OTHER PEOPLE

Roosevelt continued to rankle with Clementine. When the names of Sarah Churchill and Elliott Roosevelt came up, the President leaned over and said: "Wouldn't it be wonderful if something happened between those two?" Clementine stiffened.

"Mr. President," she huffed. "I have to point out to you that they are both married to other people."

Roosevelt got some respite on September 6, when Churchill traveled up to Massachusetts to be given an honorary degree from Harvard. Roosevelt put pressure on the president of his old university, James Conant, to lay on a ceremony "up to English standards in pomp and color."

Churchill said: "The President was very anxious for me to keep a longstanding appointment and receive an honorary degree at Harvard. It was to be an occasion for a public declaration to the world of Anglo-American unity and amity." In his acceptance speech, he said:

> *The last time I attended a ceremony of this character was in the spring of 1941, when, as Chancellor of Bristol University, I conferred a degree upon the United States Ambassador, Mr. Winant, and in absentia upon President Conant, our President, who is here today and presiding over this ceremony …*

He painted the scene:

> *… The blitz was running hard at that time, and the night before, the raid on Bristol had been heavy. Several hundreds had been killed and wounded. Many houses were destroyed. Buildings next to the University were still burning, and many of the University authorities who conducted the ceremony had pulled on their robes over uniforms begrimed and drenched; but all was presented with faultless ritual and appropriate decorum, and I sustained a very strong and invigorating impression of the superiority of man over the forces that can destroy him.*

Then he described the scene he saw in front of him at Harvard:

> *I see uniforms on every side. I understand that nearly the whole energies of the University have been drawn into the preparation of American youth for the battlefield.*

He stressed the commonality of "law, language, [and] literature" between Britain and the United States, reminding his audience that "if we, the English-Speaking peoples are together, nothing is impossible."

V-FOR-VICTORY SIGNS

Traveling back to Washington with Churchill by train, Permanent Under-Secretary for Foreign Affairs Alexander Cadogan observed:

> *Winston enjoyed himself hugely, making V-signs from the train window at all the engine drivers on the line and at all the passers-by. He quite unnecessarily rushes out on to the rear platform of the car, in a flowered silk dressing-gown, to attract and chat with anyone he can find on the platform at stopping-places. Makes Clemmie and Mary do the same—only they are conventionally dressed!*

When Roosevelt left for Hyde Park on September 10, he asked Churchill to use the White House not only as a residence but for any conference he might want to hold.

"I availed myself of these generous facilities," said Churchill and he called a meeting to review the military situation in Italy and the Pacific. Calling the meeting to order, he said: "All I want is compliance with my wishes, after reasonable discussion."

Churchill visited Roosevelt in Hyde Park again before he headed home. While there, he and Clementine celebrated their thirty-fifth wedding anniversary. Roosevelt laid on a small supper with cocktails and sherry by the fireplace. Daisy Suckley gave Mary Churchill *The True Story of Fala*, a book on the President's Scottie she had co-authored. She also recalled:

The P.M. remarked on how well the P. looked—we all agreed that it was extraordinary—It seems as though the trials & difficulties of the office of President, in these days, act as a stimulant to the P. They may take the place of the exercise which he can't have like other people.

After toasting Churchill, Roosevelt drove them to the train. As they climbed aboard, Roosevelt promised to visit England the following spring. Onboard the train taking them back to Quebec, Churchill wrote:

My dear Franklin, … We have all greatly enjoyed this trip, and I cannot tell you what a pleasure it has been to me, to Clemmie and to Mary to receive your charming hospitality at the White House and at Hyde Park. You know how I treasure the friendship with which you have honoured me and how profoundly I feel that we might together do something really fine and lasting for our two countries and, through them, for the future of all. Yours ever, W.

Roosevelt replied: "Delighted you are all safely home, and I hope you had a smooth run. All is quiet here. Congress has been here for a week and it is still quiet. My best to all three of you."

127

Daisy Suckley and FDR's dog Fala at Top Cottage in Hyde Park, New York. Photograph by Franklin D. Roosevelt.

Winston Churchill and Franklin D. Roosevelt
meeting in Quebec, Canada.

PART FOUR

OUR BAND OF BROTHERS

*It is the Germans who will suffer …
when our band of brothers gets among them.*
Winston Churchill about D-Day

CHAPTER 14

LET NOT YOUR HEART BE TROUBLED

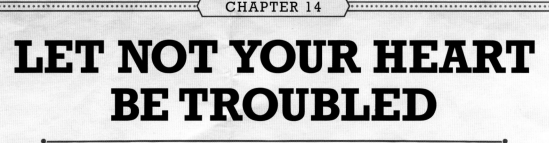

Roosevelt and Churchill met again on November 22, 1943, in Cairo, Egypt, with Generalissimo Chiang Kai-shek. When Churchill set off onboard HMS *Renown*, he had a cold in the head and a sore throat.

Onboard the USS *Iowa*, Roosevelt cabled: "It will be grand to see you again. I hope the cold is better." Churchill was now code naming the seaborne President jokingly "Admiral Queen." Roosevelt was a little concerned about meeting in Cairo as their presence was bound to be known by the enemy. He suggested moving the conference to Khartoum, but Churchill was sure that the large concentration of British forces in Cairo made it safe enough and cabled: "See St. John, chapter 14, verses 1 to 4," referring to the New Testament of the King James Bible:

> 1) *Let not your heart be troubled: ye believe in God, believe also in me.*
>
> 2) *In my Father's house are many mansions: if it were not so, I would have told you. I go to prepare a place for you.*
>
> 3) *And if I go and prepare a place for you, I will come again, and receive you unto myself; that where I am, there ye may be also.*
>
> 4) *And whither I go ye know, and the way ye know.*

After the message was sent, Churchill began to have second thoughts, and later wrote:

The Cairo Conference, Egypt, 1943. Seated left to right: Chiang Kai-shek, Roosevelt, Churchill, and Mrs. Chiang Kai-shek.

On reading this through more carefully after it had gone, I was a little concerned lest, apart from a shadow of unintended profanity, it should be thought I was taking too much upon myself and thus giving offence. However, the President brushed all objections aside and our plans were continued, unchanged.

Clementine warned Churchill, who was annoyed that the Americans had not supported the British when the Germans had forced them off the island of Leros in the eastern Mediterranean the previous week, to be careful around Roosevelt.

"I often think of your saying that the only worse thing than Allies is not having Allies," she said. Churchill was accompanied by his daughter Sarah, who was immediately charmed by Roosevelt. "One knew, of course, of his physical handicap, but after two minutes one never thought of it again," she said.

EYES BRIGHT WITH TEARS

Churchill asked Sarah to arrange a car to take them out to the Sphinx and the Pyramids, to see how close they could get. "I want to take the President, but I don't want to raise his hopes if we can't get close enough," he said.

Once he had discovered that it was possible, he raced back to tell Roosevelt: "Mr. President, you simply must come and see the Sphinx and the Pyramids. I've arranged it all."

Caught up in Churchill's infectious enthusiasm, Roosevelt leaned forward on the arms of his chair, tried to rise, then remembered he could not and sank back.

"It was a painful moment," said Sarah.

Churchill said that they would wait for him outside in the car. When Roosevelt emerged, Sarah noted, "his eyes were bright with tears."

WE CAST CARE ASIDE

Thanksgiving fell during their stay in Cairo, and Roosevelt brought turkeys.

"Let us make it a family affair," Roosevelt said to Churchill, and the two men dined with Sarah, Elliott Roosevelt, son-in-law John Boettiger, and Harry and Robert Hopkins.

"Harry had arranged an army band to play in the balcony of the drawing room," Boettiger wrote to his wife Anna Roosevelt. "We had several cocktails before dinner, then went in and there was champagne."

Churchill also recalled the Thanksgiving dinner:

We had a pleasant and peaceful feast. Two enormous turkeys were brought in with all ceremony. The President, propped up high in his chair, carved for all with masterly, indefatigable skill. As we were above twenty, this took a long time, and those who were helped first had finished before the President had cut anything for himself.

He was impressed that, by the time Roosevelt had finished the carving, he had left nothing but the carcasses. After toasting Churchill, Roosevelt explained the origins of the feast and was delighted that American troops were now spreading it throughout the world, while he was pleased to share this one with the Prime Minister.

Churchill rose to respond at this stage, but the President told him that he had still another toast first. The President then went on to say that large families are usually more closely united than small families and that, this year, with the United Kingdom in their family, they are a large family and more united than ever before. Diplomatic documents noted that "the Prime Minister responded in his usual masterful and inspiring manner."

"Upon this happy note, we all retired to the drawing room for more music: 'Carry Me Back to Old Virginny,' 'Marching Through Georgia' and similar tunes," said Boettiger.

Sarah's dance card was full, so Churchill—much to Roosevelt's amusement—asked General Edwin M. "Pa" Watson, the President's senior military aid, to dance with him.

"It is an enormous satisfaction to have my mess crew from the Potomac and Shangri-La. Music by an army band, later W.S.C. cakewalked with Pa Watson," Roosevelt wrote in his diary.

"For a couple of hours we cast care aside," Churchill said.

THE BIG THREE

Next they moved on to Tehran where the "Big Three"—Churchill, Roosevelt, and Stalin—were to meet for the first time. The Iranian capital was not the most secure venue. In August and September 1941, Britain and the Soviet Union had invaded Iran. Although regarded as neutral, it was thought that the Shah and his inner circle were sympathetic to the Axis. The Shah even pleaded with Roosevelt to intervene. The US did nothing, so the Shah was toppled and replaced by his 21-year-old son Mohammad Reza Pahlavi. However, it was decided to hold the conference in Tehran to suit Stalin who was unwilling to stray far from the borders of the Soviet Union, or travel by plane.

Driving in from the airport, Churchill's car got stuck in traffic. Sarah feared that there may be an assassin in the crowd that pressed around the car. But Churchill staged a charm offensive.

"I grinned at the crowd, and on the whole they grinned at me," he said.

When he reached the British legation, he ordered a tightening of security. He had wanted Roosevelt to stay there with him, but the President wanted his own headquarters in the American embassy. When that was found to be insecure, he accepted Stalin's invitation to move into the Soviet embassy where the talks would take place.

CHURCHILL OBEYS ORDERS

Churchill then requested a meeting with Roosevelt before the Big Three got together. Roosevelt declined as he wanted to see Stalin on his own first, figuring that he would get on with the Marshal better if Churchill was not there. Roosevelt was also wary that Churchill would press him to support an invasion of Rhodes, and then to open the Dardanelles at the cost of delaying the cross-Channel invasion of France.

Averell Harriman had to take the bad news to Churchill who had lost his voice and was not in the best of moods.

"He said that he was glad to obey orders," said Harriman, but "he had a right to be chairman of the meeting, because of his age, because his name began with C and because of the historic importance of the British Empire which he represented."

THE SHIFTING BALANCE OF POWER

Lieutenant General Sir Ian Jacob, military assistant secretary to the British War Cabinet noted:

By the time we got to the Tehran conference, one noticed that things were changing. The American power was building up. Up to that point there were just as many British forces involved in all these things as there were American, but not so in the future. And it was becoming clear also to Roosevelt that at the end of the war there would be only two great powers in existence—Russia and America ... So from that moment on, we were nothing like so close as we had been.

Lieutenant General Sir Ian Jacob (1899 – 1993).

The request was facetious.

"He waived all these claims but insisted on one thing," said Harriman, "which was that he should be allowed to give a dinner party on the 30th, which was his 69th birthday. He said he would get thoroughly drunk and be prepared to leave the next day."

At 3 p.m., Stalin called on Roosevelt, who said he had long wished to meet him in person. Stalin said the delay was "entirely due to his preoccupation with military matters." The Red Army had broken the Germans on the Eastern Front at Stalingrad and had won a massive tank battle at Kursk, partly, by intelligence passed to the Soviets by the British from their Enigma decrypts.

ENCOUNTERING JOSEPH STALIN

The first meeting of the Big Three was to take place in the large conference room in the Soviet Embassy. It had been provided with a specially-made oval table, so there would be no arguing about who was sitting at the head or the foot. When Churchill arrived shortly before 4:30 p.m., the other two were already there.

Roosevelt had been designated chairman. As the youngest of the three, Roosevelt welcomed his elders and asked Stalin to speak first. Stalin declined, saying he would rather listen. So Roosevelt began emphatically:

We are sitting around this table for the first time as a family, with the one object of winning the war. Regarding the conduct of naval and military meetings, it has been our habit, between the British and the United States, to publish nothing but to speak our minds very freely. In such a large family circle we hope that we will be very successful and achieve constructive accord in order that we may maintain close touch throughout the war and after the war.

Churchill spoke next, pointing out that the three of them represented the "greatest concentration of worldly power that had ever been seen in the history of mankind. In our hands here is the possible certainty of shortening the war, the much greater certainty of victories, but the absolute certainty that we hold the happy future of mankind."

Stalin was more perfunctory. He spoke of the "potential collaboration" of the three Allies, then thundered: "Now let us get down to business."

Joseph Stalin (1879 – 1953) was the revolutionary leader of Russia during World War II, and governed the Soviet Union from the mid-1920s until his death in 1953.

THE DISAGREEABLE BODY OF WATER

Roosevelt wanted to solicit Stalin's help in fighting the Japanese, but Stalin said he was too deeply involved in Europe. Once Germany was defeated though, he would join the war against Japan. Roosevelt then reaffirmed the decision made at the Quebec summit, that the cross-Channel invasion of France would take place in May 1944—the harsh realities of the weather would preclude a crossing before late spring. "The Channel is such a disagreeable body of water," Roosevelt added.

"We were very glad it was a disagreeable body of water at one time," said Churchill.

He went on to say that the British and American governments were fully committed to the cross-Channel invasion, now code named Overlord. By the late spring or summer of 1944, they would have accumulated thirty-five divisions. Churchill recalled saying:

The late spring and summer of 1944 were still six months away however, and the President and I had been asking ourselves what could

be done during these six months with the resources available in the Mediterranean that would best take the weight off Russia, without postponing Overlord for more than perhaps a month or two.

Roosevelt made it clear that he did not favor delaying Overlord, while Churchill added that he hoped the President would be more flexible. Stalin dismissed Italy as a sideshow. Churchill replied that, while the allies were "all great friends," they should not delude themselves into believing that they saw eye to eye on all matters.

THE GROWING BOND

That evening Roosevelt hosted dinner. He handed one of his martinis to Stalin who was not impressed.

"It is cold on the stomach," he complained. Nevertheless a bond was growing between the two men. And later Roosevelt told Daisy Suckley:

Churchill presenting Stalin with the specially-commissioned ceremonial saber, named the Sword of Stalingrad.

When I first got to Tehran, Stalin came to call on me. Of course, I did not get up when he came into the room. We shook hands, and he sat down, and I caught him looking curiously at my legs and ankles. Later, I entertained him at dinner, and was sitting at the table when he and the others came in. When Stalin was seated, on my right, he turned to the interpreter and said: "Tell the President that I now understand what it has meant for him to make the effort to come on such a long journey. Tell him that the next time I will go to him."

Of course, Stalin did not ever go to America. Their next meeting would be at Yalta on Soviet soil in the Crimea.

Over steak, Stalin launched an attack on the French for having capitulated so easily and ventured that it would be wrong to return their empire to them. Churchill protested that he could not conceive of a civilized world without a flourishing France, but being an anti-colonialist Roosevelt said he was in part agreement with Stalin.

Stalin moved on to Germany, which he thought should be dismembered and suffer the harshest possible treatment to prevent the resurgence of German militarism. The working class there were too timid to challenge authority, he said. Roosevelt was about to respond when he fell ill. He was taken to his room where his doctor diagnosed a severe case of indigestion.

Churchill and Stalin returned to the conference room where, it was noted, Churchill did most of the talking. While Roosevelt had intelligently learned to keep his points short and pithy when communicating through a translator, Churchill continued as long-winded as ever, leaving the listener waiting for extended passages of speech to be translated.

THE SWORD OF STALINGRAD

As Churchill knew that, staying in the same building, Roosevelt and Stalin would be having private conversations, he suggested that he and Roosevelt lunch together the next day, before the plenary session in the afternoon. Roosevelt

declined. Churchill was surprised, saying: "I thought we all three should treat each other with equal confidence."

This was more than a snub. Churchill noted: "The President after luncheon had a further interview with Stalin and [Soviet Foreign Minister Vyacheslav] Molotov, at which many important matters were discussed, including particularly Mr. Roosevelt's plan for the government of the post-war world."

As always, Churchill had a trick up his sleeve. Before the talks resumed, he presented Stalin with a specially-commissioned ceremonial saber, named the Sword of Stalingrad, honoring Stalin's resistance to Hitler. Stalin raised it to his lips and kissed the blade.

On the second day of talks, the differences erupted. Stalin demanded to know who was going to command Overlord. Roosevelt explained that a final choice had not been made yet, though a leader candidate, George Marshall, was at the conference.

"Then nothing will come out of these operations," Stalin fumed.

He then took on Churchill, asking: "Do the British really believe in Overlord, or are you only saying so to reassure the Russians?"

"It will be our stern duty to hurl across the Channel against the Germans every sinew of our strength," Churchill replied.

GOADING CHURCHILL

That evening, it was Stalin's turn to host dinner. There were cold hors d'oeuvres to start with, then hot borscht, fish, a selection of meats, salad, compotes, and fruits, accompanied by vodka and fine wines, and numerous toasts. During the meal, Stalin missed no opportunity to goad Churchill, even suggesting that he was nursing a secret affection for the Germans and wanted a "soft" peace. Churchill was tired and did not respond. Nor did Roosevelt come to his aid by pointing out that Churchill had stood up to Hitler while Stalin had signed a pact with him.

Stalin went on to say that, at the end of the war, the German General Staff were to be liquidated and fifty thousand officers and technicians should be rounded up and shot.

"The British Parliament and public will never tolerate mass executions," Churchill said. "Even if in war passion they allowed them to begin, they would turn violently against those responsible after the first butchery had taken place. The Soviets must be under no delusion on this point."

Stalin was insistent: "Fifty thousand."

"I would rather be taken out into the garden here and now and be shot myself than sully my own and my country's honor by such infamy," Churchill countered.

At last Roosevelt stepped in, with a compromise. Only "49,000 should be shot," he said.

Elliott Roosevelt, slightly the worse for champagne, tottered to his feet and said that, not only did he agree with Marshal Stalin's plan, he was sure that the US Army would too. Churchill stormed from the room in frustration. In the darkness of the corridor outside, Churchill was cooling off:

> I had not been there a minute before hands were clapped upon my shoulders from behind,

> and there was Stalin, with Molotov at his side, both grinning broadly, and eagerly declaring that they were only playing, and that nothing of a serious character had entered their heads.

But Churchill was far from convinced:

> Stalin has a very captivating manner when he chooses to use it, and I never saw him do so to such an extent as at that moment … I consented to return, and the rest of the evening passed pleasantly.

SHARING WITH STALIN

Not only had Roosevelt not come to Churchill's aid in the engagement, he had rather enjoyed it. He told the cabinet later: "Joe teased the PM like a boy and it was very amusing." Finding Roosevelt and Stalin ganging up on him, Churchill responded in kind:

> The fact that the President was in private contact with Marshal Stalin and dwelling at the Soviet Embassy, and that he had avoided

Soviet World War II poster, 1942, depicting Hitler being strangled by Russian, British, and American hands.

ever seeing me alone since we left Cairo, in spite of our hitherto intimate relations and the way in which our vital affairs were interwoven, led me to seek a direct personal interview with Stalin.

This was arranged, but Churchill had more thoughts on the matter:

I began by reminding the Marshal that I was half American and had a great affection for the American people. What I was going to say was not to be understood as disparaging to the Americans, and I would be perfectly loyal towards them, but there were things which it was better to say outright between two persons.

Churchill shared his concerns about the Americans with Stalin. Firstly, there were two or three times as many British troops in the Mediterranean and he did not want his armies there hamstrung. Secondly, the Americans were pressing him to undertake an amphibious operation in the Bay of Bengal against the Japanese in March, which he was not keen on. Meanwhile he was pressing Roosevelt to make a decision on who should command Overlord—after conceding that it should be an American, while the British would retain command in the Mediterranean. Churchill remembered Stalin's response:

Stalin said he must warn me that the Red Army was depending on the success of our invasion of Northern France. If there were no operations in May 1944, then the Red Army would think that there would be no operations at all that year. The weather would be bad and there would be transport difficulties. If the operation did not take place, he did not want the Red Army to be disappointed. Disappointment could only create bad feeling. If there was no big change in the European war in 1944, it would be very difficult for the Russians to carry on. They were war-weary.

There was an implicit threat in this response, that Stalin might make a separate peace with Hitler.

PLEASED AND RELIEVED

The two of them then moved to Roosevelt's quarters for lunch, where the President confirmed that Overlord should go ahead in May 1944.

"The Marshal was evidently greatly pleased and relieved by this solemn and direct engagement which we both made," said Churchill. That night dinner was to be held in the British Legation as Churchill explained:

This could not well be disputed. Great Britain and myself both came first alphabetically, and in seniority I was four or five years older than Roosevelt or Stalin. We were by centuries the longest established of the three Governments; I might have added, but did not, that we had been the longest in the war; and finally, November 30 was my birthday.

The table was set with crystal and silver that glinted in candlelight. Roosevelt and Churchill wore black tie, while Stalin was in uniform. "Glasses were never permitted to stand empty and the champagne consumed would float a battleship," wrote John Boettiger.

Stalin sat on Churchill's left, Roosevelt on his right. For the moment, it seemed that the enmity of the last three days had been forgotten. Stalin rose to thank Roosevelt for the shipments that were keeping the Red Army alive and fighting. Without Lend-Lease, he acknowledged, "we would lose this war." Then it was Churchill's turn to speak:

Together we controlled practically all the naval and three-quarters of all the air forces in the world, and could direct armies of nearly twenty millions of men, engaged in the most terrible of wars that had yet occurred in human history ... I could not help rejoicing at the long way we had come on the road to victory since the summer of 1940, when we had been alone, and, apart from the Navy and the Air Force, practically unarmed, against the triumphant and unbroken might of Germany and Italy, with almost all Europe and its resources in their grasp.

Roosevelt had the last word. At 2 a.m., he triumphantly raised his glass and said:

We have differing customs and philosophies and ways of life. But we have proved here at Tehran that the varying ideals of our nations can come together in a harmonious whole, moving unitedly for the common good of ourselves and of the world.

THE ODD MAN OUT

Roosevelt was a little uncomfortable that he had scarcely seen Churchill alone during the conference, but it was his purpose to establish a personal rapport with Stalin so that it would be easier to deal with him later by telephone, cable, or letter. So he came up with a plan. Later he told Frances Perkins:

On my way to the conference room that morning we caught up with Winston and I just had a moment to say to him, "Winston. I hope you won't be sore at me for what I am going to do."

Winston just shifted his cigar and grunted. I must say he behaved very decently afterward.

I began almost as soon as we got into the conference room. I talked privately with Stalin. I didn't say anything that I hadn't said before, but it appeared quite chummy and confidential, enough so that the other Russians joined us to listen. Still no smile.

Then I said, lifting my hand to cover a whisper (which of course had to be interpreted), "Winston is cranky this morning, he got up on the wrong side of the bed."

A vague smile passed over Stalin's eyes, and I decided I was on the right track. As soon as I sat down at the conference table, I began to tease Churchill about his Britishness, about John Bull, about his cigars, about his habits. It began to register with Stalin. Winston got red and scowled, and the more he did so, the more Stalin smiled. Finally Stalin broke out into a deep, heavy guffaw, and for the first time in three days I saw light. I kept it up until Stalin was laughing with me, and it was then that I called him "Uncle Joe." He would have thought me fresh the day before, but that day

he laughed and came over and shook my hand.

From that time on our relations were personal, and Stalin himself indulged in an occasional witticism. The ice was broken and we talked like men and brothers.

Less than three hours later, Roosevelt and Stalin had another private meeting. They discussed the fate of Poland, with Roosevelt reminding Stalin that there were between six and seven million Americans of Polish extraction and, as a practical man, he did not want to lose their votes.

Although Roosevelt said that Churchill "behaved very decently afterward," Churchill's daughter Mary said her father was very hurt.

"My father was awfully wounded at Tehran," she said. "For reasons of state, it seems to me President Roosevelt was out to charm Stalin, and my father was the odd man out. He felt that very keenly."

"I love that man," Churchill told his doctor, the recently ennobled Lord Moran, in conversation with him about the President.

RETURN TO CAIRO

Roosevelt and Churchill traveled back via Cairo together where Roosevelt announced that Eisenhower would command Overlord. By then, Churchill's cold had turned into pneumonia. He ended up convalescing in Marrakech, in the villa he had stayed in with Roosevelt after the Casablanca conference. He said he could never remember being so tired and did not even have the strength to paint.

"Even tottering from the motor-car to a picnic luncheon in lovely weather amid the foothills of the Atlas was limited to eighty or a hundred yards," he said. "I passed eighteen hours out of the twenty-four supine."

But Clementine could not stop him working, and she was resigned to it. "I never think of after the war," she told a friend. "I think Winston will die when it is over."

Back in the States after Tehran, Roosevelt said to White House speechwriter Sam Rosenman: "Winston has developed a tendency to make long speeches which are repetitious of long speeches which he has made before."

Churchill had a similar criticism of Roosevelt. Recuperating in Marrakech, he said to Tommy Thompson: "Tommy, you will bear witness that I do not repeat my stories so often as my dear friend, the President of the United States."

WE GOT ALONG FINE

On Christmas Eve 1943, Roosevelt broadcast one of his fireside chats from Hyde Park. Though he mentioned Stalin, Chiang Kai-shek, and others, he added a personal note about Churchill:

> *Of course, as you all know, Mr. Churchill and I have happily met many times before, and we know and understand each other very well. Indeed, Mr. Churchill has become known and beloved by many millions of Americans, and the heartfelt prayers of all of us have been with this great citizen of the world in his recent serious illness.*

There was some flattery for Stalin too.

> *To use an American and somewhat ungrammatical colloquialism, I may say that I "got along fine" with Marshal Stalin. He is a man who combines a tremendous, relentless determination with a stalwart good humor. I believe he is truly representative of the heart and soul of Russia; and I believe that we are going to get along very well with him and the Russian people—very well indeed.*

He also mentioned that the coalition—Britain, Russia, China, and the United States and their allies—now represented more than three-quarters of the total population of the earth.

The Roosevelt family at home on Christmas Eve, 1943. Although the president had faced a battery of microphones to tell the world of invasion plans, he also celebrated a typical family night-before-Christmas surrounded by his children and grandchildren.

CHAPTER 15

D-DAY—THE INVASION OF EUROPE

As the planning for the D-Day landings went ahead, both Roosevelt and Churchill knew they were taking a huge political gamble. Roosevelt faced another election in November 1944. If anything went wrong with the invasion of Europe, the door would be open for the Republicans.

Similarly Churchill had already faced two votes of no confidence and ferocious criticism after the fall of Singapore and Tobruk.

Having returned to England onboard the battleship *King George V*, Churchill wrote to Roosevelt on January 18, 1944:

> *I have now got home again safely and am all right except for being rather shaky on my pins. I must thank you for the delightful stay we had at flower villa and for the princely hospitality which you extended to me through the American Army. I was very much tempted to remain for another fortnight but thought it my duty to return on account primarily of Shingle.*

Operation Shingle was originally conceived by Churchill in December 1943, as he lay recovering from pneumonia in Marrakech. His plan was to land two divisions at Anzio, bypassing German forces holding a defensive line in central Italy, and take Rome.

In early February, Harry Hopkins' son Stephen, age 18, was killed in action in the Marshall Islands, between Hawaii and the Philippines in the central Pacific. Roosevelt cabled Hopkins, who was recuperating in Florida:

THE DEATH OF STEPHEN HOPKINS

Churchill sent Harry Hopkins a scroll of parchment with a quote from the last scene of *Macbeth* hand-lettered on it:

> Stephen Peter Hopkins
>
> Age 18
>
> Your son, my lord, has paid a soldier's debt.
>
> He only liv'd but till he was a man,
>
> The which no sooner had his prowess confirm'd
>
> In the unshrinking station where he fought,
>
> But like a man he died.
>
> Shakespeare.
>
> To Harry Hopkins from Winston S. Churchill
>
> 13 February, 1944.

Harry Hopkins with Prime Minister Winston Churchill.

I am terribly distressed to have to tell you that Stephen was killed in action at Kwajalein. We have no details as yet other than that he was buried at sea. His mother has been notified. I am confident that when we get details we will all be even prouder of him than ever. I am thinking of you much. FDR.

Churchill also wrote to Hopkins: "Dear Harry, Please accept our most profound sympathy with you in your honor and grief. Winston and Clementine Churchill."

WORN OUT BY THE WAR

In England, on February 17, 1944, the Conservative candidate William Cavendish lost an acrimonious by-election in West Derbyshire by over 4,500 votes to an independent candidate Charles White from the short-lived Common Wealth Party. It was a defeat for the coalition government, and Churchill took it badly.

"Sitting in a chair in his study," said Jock Colville, "the PM looked old, tired and very depressed and was even muttering about a General Election." Roosevelt was not making a good showing in the polls either. His re-election was so important to Churchill that he sent Beaverbrook over to assess his chances. Joseph Kennedy told him that he was certain that Roosevelt would be defeated. One of the criticisms of the President was that he had followed Churchill's strategy in 1942 and 1943.

Wendell Willkie, Beaverbrook noted, was "moving in the direction of hostility to Great Britain's public men." The most likely Republican nominee, the Governor of New York Thomas E. Dewey, "was of the opinion that the war is nearly over," so confined himself to domestic issues. Returning to London, Beaverbrook told Churchill of the "danger of hurting Roosevelt by coming up too strongly in his favor." All he could do was pray.

Between January and April 1944, the Germans renewed the bombing of London. On February 21, Churchill cabled Roosevelt: "We have just had a stick of bombs around

10 Downing Street and there are no more windows. Clemmie and I were at Chequers and luckily all the servants were in the shelter. Four persons killed outside."

Roosevelt was also worn out by the war. To revive his spirits his old flame Lucy Mercer was invited to Hyde Park soon after her husband Winthrop Rutherfurd died. A medical check-up diagnosed, among other things, hypertension, hypertensive heart disease, cardiac failure in the left ventricle, and acute bronchitis. This worried Churchill. Chief of the Imperial General Staff General Alan Brooke recorded in his war diaries on May 7:

He looked very old and very tired. He said Roosevelt was not well and that he was no longer the man he had been; this, he said, also applied to himself. He said he could still always sleep well, eat well and especially drink well! but that he no longer jumped out of bed the way he used to, and felt as if he would be quite content to spend the whole day in bed. I have never yet heard him admit that he was beginning to fail.

OPERATION OVERLORD

While Roosevelt took a rest, Churchill's therapy was to throw himself into the planning of Operation Overlord. In a meeting in Downing Street in the small hours of the morning, staff were discussing when exactly they should make the crossing. After the discussion seemed to be getting nowhere, Churchill demanded to know when William the Conqueror had made his crossing.

General Ismay, who was standing behind Churchill, coughed politely and said: "Sir, I think it was 1066."

"Damn it, everybody knows it was 1066," he said, banging his fist on the table. "I want to know what month and what day."

When none of his officers could tell him, he said: "Class dismissed."

It turned out that the Norman fleet had set sail on September 27. This was too late in the year for Stalin or Roosevelt. Nevertheless, Churchill was now brimming with confidence.

On April 12, he cabled Roosevelt:

On Good Friday [April 7] I gave a talk to all the generals, British and American, who gathered at General Montgomery's headquarters, expressing my strong confidence in the result of this extraordinary but magnificent operation. I understand you have received some account of this from General Eisenhower, Mr. McCloy and General McNarney who were present. I do not agree with the loose talk which has been going on on both sides of the Atlantic about the undue heavy casualties which we shall sustain. In my view it is the Germans who will suffer very heavy casualties when our band of brothers gets among them.

A PICTURE OF THE PM

On May 20, Roosevelt sent a letter thanking Churchill for a portrait he had sent. It arrived just before D-Day:

Hyde Park, N.Y.

May 20, 1944

Dear Winston:—

That picture of you I particularly like. So much so that it too becomes an inhabitant of my bedroom wall. I am awfully glad to have it.

I am safely back in Washington trying to catch up and I am really practically all right again though I am still having some tests made on my plumbing and am keeping regular hours with much allocation to sleep. The old bronchial pneumonia has completely disappeared. The real triumph is that I have lost nearly ten pounds in the last couple of months and now I have begun the struggle to maintain the loss.

I do not believe I can get away for over a month. Of course, I am greatly disappointed that I could not be in England just at this moment, but perhaps having missed the boat it will be best not to make the trip until the events of the near future are more clear.

I got awfully good reports of you from Averell and Winant. Remember what I told old Moran to make you do—obey his orders. Thus the Commander-in-Chief in one country orders around a mere Minister of Defense in another country.

At this writing the news from Italy looks good. I hope Alec [General Sir Harold Alexander, Commander-in-Chief of all Allied Forces in Italy] keeps up the good work.

With my affectionate regards,

Churchill cabled a reply:

I was so glad to get your charming letter of May 20th. Our friendship is my greatest stand-by amid the ever-increasing complications of this exacting war. Averell brought me a good account of your physical health, and I have sustained from many quarters impressions that your political health is also greatly improved … I am here near Ike's Headquarters in my train. His main pre-occupation is the weather. There are wonderful sights to see with all these thousands of vessels.

Portrait of Sir Winston Churchill.

GRAVE AND TERRIBLE DECISIONS OF WAR

On April 25, Colville noted that, when it came to the landings, Churchill "would be among the first, he said, if he possibly could—and what fun it would be to get there before Monty." General Montgomery had been appointed commander of the ground forces during the invasion, now planned for June 5. The day before, Rome became the first Axis capital to fall to the Allies after the success of Operation Shingle and victory at the battle of Anzio, and Roosevelt cabled: "We have just heard of the fall of Rome and I am about to drink a mint julep to your good health … The whole operation was a magnificent example of perfect teamwork."

Eisenhower said that he could not take responsibility for Churchill going to France with the D-Day landings, and it took two strongly-worded letters from King George VI to finally dissuade him. He eventually made it to the beaches on June 12, when the bridgehead in Normandy was still only a matter of a few miles deep and still under intermittent shellfire, and occasional air attack, but he regretted missing the main event. In his memoirs, he recorded:

> *A man who has to play an effective part in taking, with the highest responsibility, grave and terrible decisions of war may need the refreshment of adventure. He may need also the comfort that when sending so many others to their death he may share in a small way their risks.*

As it was he had to content himself with a visit to Eisenhower's headquarters near Portsmouth in southern England when the invasion, delayed by bad weather, eventually went ahead on June 6, 1944. He commandeered a train so he would have somewhere nearby to work and sleep.

An American armored group enters the city limits of Rome, Italy, June 5, 1944.

General Montgomery guides Winston Churchill to his jeep after he had come ashore to begin his tour of Normandy, June 12, 1944.

A BROTHERHOOD IN ARMS

On the night of June 5, Churchill and Clementine dined alone in 10 Downing Street—a rare occurrence. "Do you realize," Churchill told her, "that by the time you wake up in the morning twenty thousand men may have been killed?"

After cocktails and dinner in the White House, Roosevelt addressed the nation on the fall of Rome then, before going to bed, briefed Eleanor on what was happening in the English Channel. It was Eleanor that brought the first news of the invasion when the War Department phoned at around three in the morning and asked to speak to the President.

At noon on June 6, Churchill went to the House of Commons and talked for ten minutes about the liberation of Rome. Then he said:

I have also to announce to the House that during the night and the early hours of this morning the first of the series of landings in force upon the European continent has taken place. In this case the liberating assault fell upon the coast of France. An immense armada of upwards of four-thousand ships, together with several thousand smaller craft, crossed the Channel. Massed airborne landings have been successfully effected behind the enemy lines, and landings on the beaches are proceeding at various points at the present time. The fire of the shore batteries has been largely quelled. The obstacles that were constructed in the sea have not proved so difficult as was apprehended. The Anglo-American Allies are sustained by about eleven-thousand first-line aircraft … The battle that has now begun will grow constantly in scale and in intensity for many weeks to come, and I shall not attempt to speculate upon its course. This I may say, however. Complete unity prevails throughout the Allied armies. There is a brotherhood in arms between us and our friends of the United States. There is complete confidence in the supreme commander, General Eisenhower, and his lieutenants, and also in the commander of the Expeditionary Force, General Montgomery. The ardor and spirit of the troops, as I saw myself, embarking in these last few days was splendid to witness … It is, therefore, a most serious time that we enter upon. Thank God, we enter upon it with our great Allies all in good heart and all in good friendship.

EISENHOWER'S COURAGE

Roosevelt was comforted by early reports of lighter than expected casualties and took time to send two typewriters to Churchill.

Eisenhower's deputy General Joseph T. McNarney had written a note to Churchill, thanking him for his hospitality. Churchill was taken by the typeface. News of this reached the President's ear and, in an accompanying note, he wrote:

My dear Winston:

I am informed that you liked the type script of a letter recently sent you by General McNarney, U.S. Army Deputy Chief of Staff. Two electric typewriters that produce this type script are being shipped without delay which I hope you will accept as a gift from me and as a symbol of the strong bond between the people of America and Great Britain.

With warm regards and best wishes.
Very sincerely yours, …

For a second time that day, Churchill addressed the House of Commons. *The New York Times* reported:

The Prime Minister, obviously enjoying his old role of war reporter, painted a glowing picture of the initial Allied successes, which he said were accomplished with "extremely little loss," although he warned that the present phase of the invasion is "a most serious time." … A great risk had to be taken with the weather, but General Eisenhower's courage is equal to all necessary decisions that have to be taken in these extremely difficult and uncontrollable matters.

General Dwight D. Eisenhower meets Churchill, dressed in his dragon dressing gown.

A PRAYER FOR D-DAY

While Churchill became a war reporter, Roosevelt turned into a pastor. He broadcast a D-Day prayer. The text was distributed beforehand so that the radio audience of around one hundred million Americans could pray along with him:

Last night, when I spoke with you about the fall of Rome, I knew at that moment that troops of the United States and our Allies were crossing the Channel in another and greater operation. It has come to pass with success thus far. And so, in this poignant hour, I ask you to join with me in prayer:

Almighty God: Our sons, pride of our nation, this day have set upon a mighty endeavor, a struggle to preserve our Republic, our religion, and our civilization, and to set free a suffering humanity.

Lead them straight and true; give strength to their arms, stoutness to their hearts, steadfastness in their faith.

They will need Thy blessings. Their road will be long and hard. For the enemy is strong. He may hurl back our forces. Success may not come with rushing speed, but we shall return again and again; and we know that by Thy grace, and by the righteousness of our cause, our sons will triumph.

They will be sore tried, by night and by day, without rest—until the victory is won. The darkness will be rent by noise and flame. Men's souls will be shaken with the violences of war.

For these men are lately drawn from the ways of peace. They fight not for the lust of conquest. They fight to end conquest. They fight to liberate. They fight to let justice arise, and tolerance and good will among all Thy people. They yearn but for the end of battle, for their return to the haven of home.

Some will never return. Embrace these, Father, and receive them, Thy heroic servants, into Thy kingdom.

And for us at home—fathers, mothers, children, wives, sisters, and brothers of brave men overseas—whose thoughts and prayers are ever with them—help us,

Almighty God, to rededicate ourselves in renewed faith in Thee in this hour of great sacrifice.

Many people have urged that I call the Nation into a single day of special prayer. But because the road is long and the desire is great, I ask that our people devote themselves in a continuance of prayer. As we rise to each new day, and again when each day is spent, let words of prayer be on our lips, invoking Thy help to our efforts.

Give us strength, too—strength in our daily tasks, to redouble the contributions we make in the physical and the material support of our armed forces.

And let our hearts be stout, to wait out the long travail, to bear sorrows that may come, to impart our courage unto our sons wheresoever they may be.

And, O Lord, give us Faith. Give us Faith in Thee; Faith in our sons; Faith in each other; Faith in our united crusade. Let not the keenness of our spirit ever be dulled. Let not the impacts of temporary events, of temporal matters of but fleeting moment let not these deter us in our unconquerable purpose.

With Thy blessing, we shall prevail over the unholy forces of our enemy. Help us to conquer the apostles of greed and racial arrogancies. Lead us to the saving of our country, and with our sister Nations into a world unity that will spell a sure peace a peace invulnerable to the schemings of unworthy men. And a peace that will let all of men live in freedom, reaping the just rewards of their honest toil.

Thy will be done, Almighty God.

Amen.

OPERATION ANVIL

Roosevelt had a copy bound in leather and sent to Churchill. For a moment, they had been of one accord, but now they clashed again. Churchill wanted to cancel Operation Anvil, which was to follow Overlord's attack on Normandy with landings in the South of France. He wanted to use the men and equipment in Italy to drive on up the peninsula and into Austria, preventing the Red Army from marching into the Balkans or, possibly, even beating them to Berlin.

He wrote a massive memo to that effect. Roosevelt replied at equal length, concluding:

> *At Tehran, we agreed upon a definite plan of attack. That plan has gone well so far. Nothing has occurred to require any change. Now that we are fully involved in our major blow, history will never forgive us if we lose precious time and lives in indecision and debate. My dear friend, I beg you let us go ahead with our plan … Finally for purely political considerations over here I would never survive even a slight setback in Overlord if it were known that fairly large forces had been diverted to the Balkans.*

Roosevelt still had an election to fight. After Churchill had read Roosevelt's cable, General Brooke feared for the worst. On June 29, 1944, he recorded:

> *Just back from meeting with Winston. I thought at first we might have trouble with him, he looked like he wanted to fight the President. However in the end we got him to agree to our outlook, which is: "All right, if you insist on being damned fools, sooner than falling out with you, which would be fatal, we shall be damned fools with you, and we shall see that we perform the role of damned fools damned well!"*

GOD WILL BE WITH US

Churchill wanted to go to Washington to make his case personally, feeling that he could still win Roosevelt around. He wrote:

> *We are deeply grieved by your telegram. There are no differences whatever between my War Cabinet colleagues and the British Chiefs of Staff. The splitting up of the campaign in the Mediterranean into two operations neither of which can do anything decisive is, in my humble and respectful opinion the first major strategic and political error for which we two have to be responsible …*
>
> *It is with the greatest sorrow that I write to you in this sense. But I am sure that if we could have met, as I so frequently proposed, we should have reached a happy agreement. I send you every personal good wish. However we may differ on the conduct of the war, my personal gratitude to you for your kindness to me and for all you have done for the cause of freedom will never be diminished.*

Roosevelt was tactful, but would not be moved, saying:

> *I appreciate deeply your clear exposition of your feelings and views on this decision we are making. My Chiefs of Staff and I have given the deepest consideration to the problem and the points you have raised. We are still convinced that the right course of action is to launch Anvil at the earliest possible moment.*

The reason he gave was that a breakout from Italy toward Austria and the Balkans would mean passing through Istria which "has bad combat terrain in the winter time—worse than southern France … I honestly believe that God will be with us as he has in Overlord and in Italy and in North Africa. I always think of my early geometry: 'A straight line is the shortest distance between two points.'"

But by then Churchill had a new problem to face. On June 13 the first of the German V-1 flying bombs fell on London. These attacks continued until October when the last V-1 launch sites within range were overrun by Allied Forces in Germany. In September they were followed by V-2 ballistic missiles carrying a 2,200-pound (1,000 kg) warhead.

A band of US troops marching up the beachhead while landing craft in rear continue to unload supplies, equipment, and men following the victorious D-Day invasion.

BAND OF BROTHERS

The original source of the phrase "band of brothers" is a line from the St. Crispin's Day speech in *Henry V*, written by William Shakespeare in 1600.

We few, we happy few, we band of brothers …

Based on the rousing speech that King Henry V gave to the English troops before victory over the French at the Battle of Agincourt on St. Crispin's Day, October 25, 1415, the speech has been a source of inspiration for several later writers including Winston Churchill whose great hero, Admiral Horatio Nelson, referred to his captains as his "band of brothers."

During World War II, Laurence Olivier boosted British morale with a radio broadcast of the whole speech from Shakespeare's play. Churchill found it so moving that he suggested Olivier produce *Henry V* as a movie, which he did in 1944.

Then in 1992, Stephen E. Ambrose used the phrase for the title of his book *Band of Brothers*, later adapted into a TV miniseries by Stephen Spielberg and Tom Hanks, about the men of Easy Company, a crack airborne rifle company in the US Army during the Allied invasion of Europe in 1944 – 45.

CHAPTER 16

EVER-MORE ENTANGLED PROBLEMS

Although the Allies had established a bridgehead in France, things were not going well. The city of Caen in Normandy, which was supposed to have been taken on the first day, June 6, 1944, held out until July 9, preventing the Allies breaking out to the east. They had yet to take a major port. The floating "Mulberry" harbors towed across the English Channel so that the troops ashore could be resupplied were damaged during a gale of June 10 – 24. When the port of Cherbourg eventually fell to the Allies on June 27, the shipping and port facilities were so badly damaged they reinforced Roosevelt's argument to proceed with Operation Anvil in the South of France.

OTHER PREOCCUPATIONS

Meanwhile in the Pacific war, US Marines were suffering heavy casualties in fierce fighting on the island of Saipan in the Marianas. At the same time, in southeast Asia the Australians were fighting in Borneo, while the British were finally pushing the Japanese back in Burma. On June 23, Churchill wrote to Roosevelt, saying:

> We have immense tasks before us. Indeed, I cannot think of any moment when the burden of the war has laid more heavily upon me or when I have felt so unequal to its ever-more entangled problems. I greatly admire the strength and courage with which you face your difficulties, especially in a year when you have, what I may venture to call, other preoccupations.

Roosevelt's major "preoccupation," of course, was the 1944 presidential race. On June 2,

Roosevelt had written to Churchill, saying: "Over here new political situations crop up every day but so far, by constant attention, I am keeping my head above water."

By this time, his health was so precarious that he could only work hard for four hours a day. He collapsed onboard a train while campaigning in California and suffered an attack of angina while making a speech onboard a warship.

A TOUGH FIGHT AHEAD

New York Governor Thomas E. Dewey won the Republican nomination by a unanimous vote. He was the youngest of the candidates and the first to have been born in the twentieth century. He came to prominence as a special prosecutor who secured the conviction of Lucky Luciano. In the campaign, he avoided military and foreign policy debates, concentrating instead on the alleged inefficiencies, corruption, and Communist influences in incumbent President Roosevelt's New Deal programs. Roosevelt responded by dropping Henry Wallace as his running mate for vice-president, replacing him with Senator Harry S. Truman of Missouri, who had earned renown for his investigation of inefficiency. It would be a tough fight ahead.

Nevertheless, Roosevelt took some time out to send Churchill some naval souvenirs concerning the Battle of Jutland (1916) when Churchill had been First Lord of the Admiralty, and "various items which relate to some early Churchills. I thought you would like to have them for your family papers." One of them, Churchill remarked in his thank-you note was a "visiting card signed by my Father in 1886 when, as you know, he was Chancellor of the Exchequer." The others concerned the wife and brother of the 1st Duke of Marlborough. The naval papers Churchill handed on to the Admiralty for their records.

A proposed summit was put off until September by Roosevelt—"This would get me back in plenty of time for the election, although that is in the lap of the Gods."

THE MARTYRDOM OF WARSAW

Churchill was growing increasingly concerned about the slow progress of the Western Allies compared to the Soviets. He told Lord Moran: "Good God, can't you see that the Russians are spreading across Europe like a tide? They

invaded Poland, and there is nothing to prevent them from marching into Turkey and Greece." But first he would have to sit back and watch what he called "the martyrdom of Warsaw."

Roosevelt and Churchill asked Stalin to intervene. Stalin blamed the Poles for staging an uprising without telling them, saying: "The Soviet Command has come to the conclusion that it must dissociate itself from the Warsaw adventure as it cannot take either direct or indirect responsibility for the Warsaw action." Churchill pointed out this was a lie, cabling Roosevelt on August 19:

> The Polish Government have reminded me that Soviet broadcasting stations have for a considerable time past repeated appeals to the Polish population to drop all caution and start a general rising against the Germans. As late as July 29, i.e. three days before the Warsaw rising began, the Moscow radio station broadcast an appeal from the Union of Polish Patriots to the population of Warsaw which, after referring to the fact that the guns of liberation were now within hearing, called upon them as in 1939 to join battle with the Germans, this time for decisive action.

THE FOREST OF THE DEAD

The Union of Polish Patriots had been formed by Polish communists in the Soviet Union in 1943 at the instigation of Stalin after he broke relations with the Polish government-in-exile in London. This followed the discovery of some 22,000 bodies in the Katyn forest after a series of mass executions of Polish nationals carried out by the NKVD (the Soviet secret police) in April and May 1940. So many bodies were exhumed by 1943 that Katyn became known as the Forest of the Dead. Russia claimed that the victims had been murdered by the Nazis in 1941 and continued to deny responsibility for the massacre until 1990.

Roosevelt and Churchill wrote to Stalin, saying: "We believe that all three of us should do the utmost to save as many of the patriots there as possible. We hope that you will drop immediate supplies and munitions to the

The mass graves discovered in the Katyn forest, Russia.

THE WARSAW UPRISING

At the end of July 1944, Warsaw, Poland, was in its fifth year of German occupation. On the Eastern Front, Germans were in full retreat after the Red Army's spring offensive. The liberation of Poland's capital seemed imminent. As they approached the city, the Soviets encouraged the Warsaw underground—the Home Army numbering around fifty thousand—to revolt.

Loyal to the Polish government-in-exile in London, it was eager to do so before the Soviets entered the city as Moscow was already preparing its own Communist-led government to take over in Poland. The Home Army attacked the German garrison on August 1 and within three days had taken over most of the city.

However, when the Red Army reached the town of Praga on the eastern bank of the Vistula River opposite Warsaw, it stopped before entering the city. The Germans were therefore able to send reinforcements unhindered by the Russians. For the next sixty-three days Warsaw was pounded by bombs and shells. Without ammunition and food, the Home Army was forced to surrender on October 2. Warsaw's population was deported and the city destroyed.

When the Soviets finally forced the Germans out of Poland, the way was open for them to install their own pro-Soviet regime on January 1, 1945. The Soviets' collusion in the destruction of Warsaw was particularly embarrassing for the British, who had gone to war over Poland in 1939. "Such was their liberation of Poland," said Churchill, "where they now rule. But this cannot be the end of the story." Communist rule in Poland was only relinquished in 1989.

Polish resistance Home Army fighting to liberate Warsaw from Nazi Germany.

patriot Poles of Warsaw, or will you agree to help our planes in doing it very quickly."

The British and US Ambassadors asked to meet Marshal Stalin over the matter and were given a statement that Churchill then forwarded to Roosevelt. It said:

> The Soviet Government cannot, of course, object to English or American aircraft dropping arms in the region of Warsaw since this is [an] American and British affair. But they decidedly object to American and British aircraft, after dropping arms in the region of Warsaw, landing on Soviet territory, since the Soviet Government do not wish to associate themselves either directly or indirectly with the adventure in Warsaw.

BURIED IN BACKYARDS AND SQUARES

Two British attempts to fly supplies from Italy were "forlorn and inadequate." Churchill obtained an eyewitness account of what was happening in the city. After giving a copy to the Soviet Ambassador in London, he cabled another to Roosevelt:

> **August 15th**. The dead are buried in backyards and squares. The food situation is continually deteriorating, but as yet there is no starvation. Today there is no water at all in the pipes. It is being drawn from the infrequent wells and house supplies. All quarters of the town are under shell fire and there are many fires. The dropping of supplies has intensified the morale. Everyone wants to fight and will fight but the uncertainty of a speedy conclusion is depressing.
>
> **August 16th**. Fighting continues to be very bitter in Warsaw. The Germans fight for every inch of ground. It is reported that in some places whole districts have been burnt and the inhabitants either shot or taken to Germany. The inhabitants continue to repeat "When we get weapons we will pay them back …"

Churchill then suggested that Roosevelt write to Stalin, saying: "We are most anxious to send American planes from England. Why should

they not land on the refueling ground which has been assigned to us behind the Russian lines without enquiry as to what they have done on the way … Unless you directly forbid it, therefore, we propose to send the planes."

Churchill added that, if Stalin did not reply, he thought that they should go ahead anyway and see what happened. "I cannot conceive that he would maltreat or detain them," Churchill said.

Roosevelt did not reply. Stalin had already been trying to take away airfields the Americans were using in the Ukraine and elsewhere, while Roosevelt was at the same time asking for the use of airfields in Siberia to attack Japan.

DELICATE MATTERS BETWEEN FRIENDS

A second conference at Quebec was due to open on September 12, 1944. Churchill told Clementine:

> This visit of mine to the President is the most necessary one that I have ever made since the very beginning as it is there that various differences that exist between the Staffs, and also between me and the American Chiefs of Staff, must be brought to a decision.

He pointed out just how serious the situation was:

> We have three armies in the field. The first is fighting under American Command in France, the second under General Alexander is relegated to a secondary and frustrated situation by the United States' insistence on this landing on the Riviera. The third on the Burmese frontier is fighting in the most unhealthy country in the world under the worst possible conditions to guard the American air line over the Himalayas into their very over-rated China. Thus two-thirds of our forces are being misemployed for American convenience, and the other third is under American command. The casualties in Burma amounted in the first six months of the year to 288,000 sick and 40,000 killed

and wounded. These are delicate and serious matters to be handled between friends in careful and patient personal discussion. I have no doubt we shall reach a good conclusion, but you will see that life is not very easy.

Returning from Italy on September 1, Churchill was ill again. His pneumonia had returned, but he was soon well enough to sail aboard the *Queen Mary*. While Roosevelt was ill and running for office, onboard ship, Churchill was contemplating an inevitable defeat in a British postwar election. Sanguine, he said: "What is good enough for the English people is good enough for me."

He also decided to say no more about Operation Anvil, which had gone ahead on August 15, though he had managed to get its name changed to Operation Dragoon. He still considered it a waste of time, but would leave the controversy to the judgment of historians. Of course, he intended to be one of those historians, and he would later write *A History of the English-Speaking Peoples*, a four volume history of Britain and its colonies. In the meantime he engaged himself in reading and playing cards onboard ship to distract him from his work.

Roosevelt traveled to Quebec by train, stopping off discreetly to see Lucy Rutherfurd on the way. He then quickly headed to Hyde Park to pick up Eleanor after Churchill had cabled, saying he was bringing Clementine.

Second Quebec Conference, September 16, 1944. Photo taken on a terrace of the Citadel of Quebec. Left to right: The Earl of Athlone (Governor General of Canada), President Franklin D. Roosevelt, Princess Alice (wife of the Governor General), and Prime Minister Winston Churchill.

BEYOND THE DREAMS OF JUSTICE

When they met at Quebec, a reporter later recalled: "The prime minister strode forward. What I remember now was the look of affection and my discovery that they addressed each other—at least at the moment—by first name ... 'Hello, Winston!' 'Hello, Franklin!'"

Eleanor was an accomplished public performer, while Clementine had to be hounded into making a broadcast—part of which was to be in French. Her preparations were interrupted by an official luncheon that involved seven courses, four wines, and several liqueurs, along with having to greet sixty-five guests. She was then pressurized into making a speech following Mrs. Roosevelt's.

Churchill had the President to himself again for more late-night sessions. Roosevelt's doctor, Admiral McIntire, who could not be present, made the President's naval aide Admiral Wilson Brown responsible for making the President hold to a reasonable night-time schedule. Admiral Brown said:

> *With this in mind, I had the bright idea of putting it up to Mr. Churchill, and sent to him through his aide, Commander Thompson, the message Dr. McIntire had given me. The party broke up that night immediately after the movies, about ten thirty. As we all moved off together toward our quarters, Mr. Churchill, his arm firmly held by Mrs. Churchill, muttered to me, "Aren't I a good boy?"*

Churchill volunteered the Royal Navy in the final struggle against Japan and again mentioned a thrust out of Italy toward Vienna. Also on the agenda was the Morgenthau Plan, a paper drawn up by US Secretary Henry Morgenthau called *Suggested Post-Surrender Program for Germany*, which would return Germany to a preindustrial, agricultural nation by taking away its industrial capacity. Churchill opposed the plan, saying that, with a deindustrialized Germany, "England would be chained to a dead body."

Morgenthau, who was present at the conference, also proposed credits to Britain totaling $6.5 billion. When it came to the signing of the loan agreement, Roosevelt suggested they sign the Morgenthau plan first. Churchill said: "What do you want me to do? Get on my hind legs and beg like Fala?" Nevertheless, he signed.

By September 14, Jock Colville said: "The conference has been going exceedingly well from our point of view and the Americans are being amenable both strategically and financially ... While going to bed the PM told me some of the financial advantages the Americans had promised us. 'Beyond the dreams of avarice,' I said. 'Beyond the dreams of justice,' he replied."

THE TOILS OF OUR FIGHTING TROOPS

After lunch on the last day of the Quebec conference, Roosevelt and Churchill were presented with honorary degrees by the Chancellor of McGill University in the sunshine on the roof of the Citadel. Both men made speeches, but Roosevelt's was scarcely audible above the clicking of cameras. Churchill's was unusually brief, but he used a statement to the press to heap praise on his meetings with his wartime ally:

I have been urging the President for several weeks to let us have another meeting. Our affairs are so intermingled, our troops are fighting in the line together, and our plans for the future are so interwoven that it is not possible to conduct these great affairs and to fulfill these large, combined plans without frequent meetings between the principals, between the heads of the Governments, and also between the high officers on each side …

[W]hen I have the rare and fortunate chance to meet the President of the United States, we are not limited in our discussions by any sphere. We talk over the whole position in every aspect—the military, economic, diplomatic, financial. All is examined. And obviously that should be so. The fact that we have worked so long together, and the fact that we have got to know each other so well under the hard stresses of war, make the solution of problems so much simpler, so swift. What an ineffectual method of conveying human thought correspondence is—even when it is telegraphed with all the rapidity and all the facilities of modern intercommunication. They are simply dead blank walls compared to personal contacts. And that applies not only to the President and the Prime Minister of Great Britain, it applies to our principal officers, who at every stage enter in the closest association and have established friendships which have greatly aided the tasks and the toils of our fighting troops.

Mrs. Eleanor Roosevelt and Mrs. Clementine Churchill as they spoke from the radio room at CBC, Quebec, Canada, 1944.

They moved on to Hyde Park, where Clementine went on long walks with Eleanor. "She loves her meals out of doors and so life at Hyde Park is a succession of picnics," Clementine wrote. She also noted how frail President Roosevelt had become in a letter to Mary Churchill:

> *The President with all his genius does not—indeed cannot (partly because of his health and partly because of his make-up)—function round the clock, like your Father. I should not think that his mind was pinpointed on the war for more than four hours a day, which is not really enough when one is a supreme war lord.*

Nevertheless, they did get a chance to discuss Tube Alloys—the atomic bomb. Some of the scientists working on the Manhattan Project wanted to publicize their work. Roosevelt and Churchill would not hear of it and signed a secret agreement which read:

> *The suggestion that the world should be informed regarding Tube Alloys, with a view to an international agreement regarding its control and use, is not accepted. The matter should continue to be regarded as of the utmost secrecy; but when a "bomb" is finally available, it might perhaps, after mature consideration, be used against the Japanese, who should be warned that this bombardment will be repeated until they surrender.*

THE TRIANGLE OF POWER

Expecting to lose the 1944 election Roosevelt made plans to make money by writing after he left the White House. Churchill wanted another meeting between the two of them and Stalin, but Roosevelt said no. He must concentrate on the election, so Churchill went to Moscow again on his own. Roosevelt drafted a cable wishing Churchill "every success." But Hopkins stopped it being sent as this would imply that Churchill had authority to speak for both of them.

Another cable was drafted instead to Stalin, reminding him of the triangle of power: "I am firmly convinced that the three of us, and only the three of us, can find the solution to the still unresolved questions. In this sense, while appreciating the Prime Minister's desire for the meeting, I prefer to regard your forthcoming talks with Churchill as preliminary to a meeting of the three of us."

Judging from Stalin's reply it was clear that Churchill had implied that he was empowered to speak for Roosevelt, following the agreements made at Quebec. Nevertheless, Churchill wrote to Clementine from Moscow, saying: "I have had very nice talks with the Old Bear. I like him the more I see him. They respect us here and I am sure they wish to work with us."

Churchill kept Roosevelt abreast of the talks, while Roosevelt inquired after his health—Churchill had been running a temperature again. In a cable on October 18, Churchill said:

> *Although I hear the most encouraging accounts from various quarters about United States politics. I feel the suspense probably far more than you do or more than I should if my own affairs were concerned in this zone. My kindest regards and warmest good wishes.*

THE PRESIDENT'S FAILING HEALTH

Out on the stump, Roosevelt toured New York's five boroughs in an open-top car in the pouring rain. Dewey was advised to challenge Roosevelt over his failing health. He decided not to, as the tour was a way to put an end to the persistent rumors.

Churchill saw pictures of the tour, but wasn't convinced. When he got back to London on October 23, he cabled:

> *I was delighted to see the proof of your robust vigor in New York. Nevertheless I cannot believe that four hours in an open car and pouring rain with a temperature of 40 and clothes wet through conform to those limits of prudence which you would be so ready to prescribe if it were my case. I earnestly hope you are none the worse and should be grateful for reassurance. I cannot think about anything except this ... election.*

Roosevelt replied: "My journey to New York was useful and rain does not hurt an old sailor. Thank you for your advice nevertheless. I am in top form for the … election."

Despite his fear that he was going to lose, Roosevelt exchanged ideas for the proposed Big Three meeting. During his broadcast on the eve of the election, he took time to draw attention to the V-2 rockets now pummeling London, saying "we must consider the devastation wrought on the people of England, for example, by the new long-range bombs."

LINCOLN QUOTATION

If I were trying to read much less answer all the attacks made on me, this shop might as well be closed for any other business. I do the best I know how, the very best I can; and I mean to keep on doing it to the end. If the end brings me out all right, what is said against me will not amount to anything. If the end brings me out all wrong, ten angels swearing I was right would make no difference.

This quotation was also read by President Warren Harding at the dedication of the Lincoln Memorial on May 30, 1922.

It was early in the morning of November 8 when Churchill received a cable from Hopkins, saying Roosevelt had won. The popular vote was close—25 million to 22 million, but in the Electoral College Roosevelt defeated Dewey by 432 to 99. Churchill cabled Roosevelt:

I always said that a great people could be trusted to stand by the pilot who weathered the storm. It is an indescribable relief to me that our comradeship will continue and will help to bring the world out of misery. I send you, as you have forgotten it, a copy of the telegram I sent you in 1940, much of which is true today.

It was the telegram that Roosevelt had not bothered to reply to four years earlier.

While Churchill usually remembered Roosevelt's birthday, Roosevelt often overlooked Churchill's. But in 1944, Churchill's seventieth, he did not. From Warm Springs, Georgia, he cabled: "Ever so many happy returns of the day. I shall never forget the party with you and UJ a year ago and we must have more of them that are even better. Affectionate regards, FDR."

A birthday present also arrived. Roosevelt had one of his favorite quotations from Abraham Lincoln transcribed and framed. It was sent to England with the message: "For Winston on his Birthday—I would go even to Tehran to be with him again."

Churchill replied:

I am deeply grateful to you for your most kind message on my birthday, which gave me the greatest pleasure, and also for the framed quotation from Abraham Lincoln with your own charming note upon it. This reached me, by sure hands, when I awoke. I cannot tell you how much I value your friendship or how much I hope upon it for the future of the world, should we both be spared.

Instead of Tehran, Roosevelt would in fact go to Yalta.

Abraham Lincoln, 16th President of the United States, with Roosevelt's favorite quotation above.

CHAPTER 17

FROM MALTA TO YALTA

Stalin had always been reluctant to leave Soviet territory and picked Yalta in the Crimea, on the southern coast of Ukraine, as the venue for the next meeting of the Big Three—with the excuse that his doctors had forbidden any more distant travel. Churchill told Roosevelt via Harry Hopkins: "We could not have found a worse place for a meeting if we had spent ten years on research."

The Red Army had only nine months earlier recaptured the Crimea from the Germans in ferocious fighting. Hopkins reported that Churchill "feels that he can survive it by bringing an adequate supply of whiskey. He claims it is good for typhus and deadly on lice which thrive in those parts."

It was Roosevelt who was really ill and only had the strength for a short conference, suggesting that it should not last more than five or six days. This upset Churchill. Jock Colville wrote on January 10, 1945:

> The P.M. remained in bed. He is disgusted that the President should want to spend only five or six days at the coming meeting between "the Big Three" and says that even the Almighty required seven to settle the world. (An inaccuracy which was quickly pointed out to him. Viz. Genesis 1.)[God rested on the seventh day]

Roosevelt and Churchill with their daughters Anna Boettiger (left) and Sarah Churchill onboard USS *Quincy* at Malta, February 2, 1945.

ONBOARD THE USS *QUINCY*

But Churchill would not be told, and later that day, he repeated the biblical error when he cabled Roosevelt, saying: "I do not see any other way of realizing our hopes about World Organization in five or six days. Even the Almighty took seven."

However, Churchill did persuade Roosevelt to have a preliminary meeting between the two of them on Malta.

"I shall be waiting on the quay," said Churchill. "Everything can be arranged to your convenience." Unable to contain himself, Churchill then added: "No more let us falter! From Malta to Yalta! Let nobody alter!"

As Churchill flew into Malta on January 30, his temperature soared to 102.5°F. But he was fortunate to make it at all—one of the three planes carrying his entourage overshot the runway and landed in the sea, killing seven.

In the morning, Churchill's fever lifted. He wrote to Clementine: "The President arrives at the first light of dawn and I shall go and see him as soon as he desires it."

They had lunch onboard the USS *Quincy*. Churchill was struck by the President's high spirits and friendly manner. "He must have noticed the candle by my bed when we were at the White House," Churchill told Moran, "because there was a small lighted candle at the luncheon table by my place to light my cigar."

THE DETRITUS OF WAR

They flew the fourteen hundred miles to the Crimea separately. Churchill's plane made a bumpy landing at Saki, where the runway had been swept of snow leaving an icy strip only just wide enough to land on. The Prime Minister then walked over to the President's plane and stood by while he was helped out. They were driven to another part of the airfield to review the guard of honor. Then they were treated to caviar, smoked sturgeon, suckling-pig, and black bread, washed down with vodka and sweet champagne.

Next they faced an eighty-mile drive in the snow over the mountains to Yalta, a route which was still strewn with the detritus of war. Roosevelt managed to get some sleep on the trip as his daughter had taken the precaution of getting him in a separate car from Churchill, who would have talked all the way.

The conference was to be held in the Livadia Palace, Yalta, the summer retreat of the last Russian tsar, Nicholas II, where apartments were set aside for Roosevelt. The Soviet delegation was housed in the Yusupov Palace near Yalta. Churchill stayed in the Vorontsov Palace at Odessa some five miles away. Stalin came to see him there.

OUT OF KINDNESS

Again Roosevelt insisted on seeing Stalin alone on the first day. They greeted each other like old friends and shook hands warmly. Roosevelt's translator Charles E. Bohlen even noticed that Stalin revealed a slight smile, a rare occurrence. Bohlen recorded in his notes:

> *The President said that he had been very much struck by the extent of German destruction in the Crimea and therefore he was more bloodthirsty in regard to the Germans than he had been a year ago, and he hoped that Marshal Stalin would again propose a toast to the execution of 50,000 officers of the German Army.*

This was the toast that had so annoyed Churchill at Tehran and Bohlen took it as a signal that Roosevelt would not be joining Churchill in any joint negotiating position. To reinforce the point:

> *The President said he would now tell the Marshal something indiscreet, since he would not wish to say it in front of Prime Minister Churchill, namely that the British for two years have had the idea of artificially building up France into a strong power which would have 200,000 troops on the eastern border of France to hold the line for the period required to assemble a strong British army. He said the British were a peculiar people and wished to have their cake and eat it too.*

However, Roosevelt did concede that France should have a zone of occupation in Germany, "only out of kindness."

THE AGONY OF THE WORLD

At dinner after the first session, Roosevelt mentioned that he and Churchill called Stalin "Uncle Joe." Stalin was offended, or feigned it. When Roosevelt mentioned that the Polish voters in the US were vitally interested in the future of Poland, Stalin was dismissive, saying: "Of your seven million Poles only seven thousand vote. I looked it up and I know I am right."

Roosevelt was too polite to gainsay him. Stalin sought to needle Churchill again. But the Prime Minister was resolute:

Though I'm constantly being beaten up as a reactionary, I'm the only representative present who can be thrown out of office at any time by the universal suffrage of my people. Personally, I glory in the danger.

Stalin remarked that Churchill seemed to fear elections. "I not only do not fear them, but I'm proud of the right of the British people to change their government any time they see fit," he retorted.

Stalin then said that he would not submit to the judgment of smaller nations. "The eagle should permit the small birds to sing," said Churchill, "and care not wherefore they sang."

This good-natured sparring went on until eleven o'clock, accompanied by large amounts of champagne. Nevertheless Churchill was often gloomy.

Roosevelt and Churchill at the Yalta Conference, when tensions began to develop between them.

"I do not suppose that at any moment in history has the agony of the world been so great or widespread," he said. "Tonight the sun goes down on more suffering than ever before in the world." Writing to Clementine, he said:

I am free to confess to you that my heart is saddened by the tales of the masses of German women and children flying along the roads everywhere in 40-mile long columns to the West before the advancing Armies. I am clearly convinced that they deserve it; but that does not remove it from one's gaze. The misery of the whole world appalls me and I fear increasingly that new struggles may arise out of those we are successfully ending.

PUZZLED AND DISTRESSED

There was genuine tension between Churchill and Roosevelt. "Winston is puzzled and distressed," said Lord Moran. "The President no longer seems to the PM to take an intelligent interest in the war; often he does not seem even to read the papers the PM gives him."

But it was a two way street. Churchill's daughter Mary said: "I suppose they became quite wearied with Papa banging on about things they didn't think were important." But Lord Moran knew Churchill's relationship with Roosevelt meant he was reluctant to give the President a hard time:

Though we have moved a long way since Winston, speaking of Roosevelt, said to me in the garden at Marrakech, "I love that man," he is still very reticent in criticism. It seems to be dragged out of him against his will. And with half a chance he will tell over dinner how many divisions the Americans had in a particular show against our handful, and how their casualties in that engagement dwarfed ours, and things of that kind.

After a very long day at the conference Roosevelt complained to aide James Byrnes: "Winston has developed a tendency to deliver long speeches which he has delivered before." Byrnes said, "Well, yes, but they were good speeches."

Roosevelt had to admit with a chuckle: "Well, Winston doesn't make any other kind."

As Churchill launched into another speech at the Livadia Palace, Secretary of State Edward Stettinius slipped Roosevelt a note saying: "Now we're in for a half hour of it."

One afternoon Churchill fell asleep at the conference table, he awoke suddenly and began making a speech about the Monroe Doctrine. The President had to tell him repeatedly that it was a very fine speech, but it was not the subject under discussion.

Roosevelt still enjoyed taking the chair at these meetings and relished the opportunity to put Churchill in his place. The Prime Minister, foreign correspondent John Gunther noted, sometimes looked "as if he were about to get hit." Roosevelt by this time was admitting he was weary:

Yes, I am tired. So would you be if you had spent the last five years pushing Winston uphill in a wheelbarrow.

NEVER A VENGEFUL OR SAVAGE WORD

Despite the antagonism, there was still a genuine affection between the two of them. George Elsey said: "When they are apart, FDR could be very emotional about Winnie, but then seconds later he'd put him down." Nevertheless Roosevelt could not help a derogatory and ironic tone creeping in when he talked about Churchill, even when he was talking to the Prime Minister's own advisors.

After a long war, Britain was exhausted and no longer the power it had been. So in discussions over Poland or the Balkans, Churchill's perspective held little sway.

"In all these arguments, the President's view carried the day," said Churchill's daughter, Mary. "Yet I never heard my father, at any time during all the stress of war, say a vengeful or savage word about the President." However, both British and American advisors admitted that their leaders were not on top form.

"Our leader was ill at Yalta," admitted Bohlen, "but he was effective."

Though Roosevelt and Churchill did their best to build a relationship with Stalin at Yalta, the conference still heralded the start of the Cold War, a geopolitical tension between East and West which lasted until the collapse of the Soviet Union in 1991.

A FRIEND WE CAN TRUST

On the last evening of the conference, Churchill led a somewhat disingenuous toast to Stalin, saying:

> *The fire of war has burnt up the misunderstandings of the past. We feel we have a friend whom we can trust, and I hope he will continue to feel the same about us. I pray he may live to see his beloved Russia not only glorious in war, but also happy in peace.*

Pointing to a map showing the German town of Cleves on the Rhine, which had just fallen to the Allies, he regaled Roosevelt and Stalin with tales of Anne of Cleves, the fourth wife of Henry VIII, before singing the World War I song "When We've Wound Up the Watch on the Rhine." Stalin then taunted Churchill that the British were looking for an earlier armistice than the Soviets wanted, so Churchill gave him a few lines from "Keep Right on to the End of the Road." Roosevelt then told the Soviet interpreter to tell Stalin that "this singing by the Prime Minister was Britain's secret weapon."

Before they left Yalta, Roosevelt, Churchill, and Stalin signed agreements on the creation of the United Nations, the dismemberment and occupation of Germany, reparations, Japan, the treatment of major war criminals, various frontier problems, and the Declaration on Liberated Europe.

A MATTER OF PROTOCOL

Roosevelt returned to USS *Quincy*, now moored in Great Bitter Lake in the Suez Canal, Egypt, where he met Emperor Haile Selassie of Ethiopia, King Ibn Saud of Arabia, and King Farouk of Egypt. Again Churchill was put out

that he was seeing the three monarchs without him. This amused Roosevelt. Churchill arrived onboard on February 15, when they discussed the atomic bomb.

They had an informal lunch and, just before Churchill was about to leave, Roosevelt presented him with an album of photographs from their meeting in Quebec in 1944. They arranged for Roosevelt to visit England in May and "bade affectionate farewells."

Not to be outdone, Churchill summoned Haile Selassie, Ibn Saud, and Farouk to see him. But there was a matter of protocol to deal with. Churchill recalled:

> *I had been told that neither smoking nor alcoholic beverages were allowed in the Royal Presence. As I was the host at luncheon I raised the matter at once, and said to the interpreter that if it was the religion of His Majesty to deprive himself of smoking and alcohol I must point out that my rule of life prescribed as an absolutely sacred rite smoking cigars and also the drinking of alcohol before, after, and if need be during all meals and in the intervals between them. The king graciously accepted the position. His own cupbearer from Mecca offered me a glass of water from its sacred well, the most delicious that I had ever tasted.*

BRITISH IMPERIALISM

Now that victory seemed pretty close and the time was drawing near to address some of the tough principles contained in the Atlantic Charter. Roosevelt was beginning to feel that the traditions of British imperialism were playing too heavy a part in Churchill's thinking, particularly when it came to British possessions in the Far East.

When asked if Churchill wanted British territories back the way they were before the war, Roosevelt said: "Yes, he is mid-Victorian on things like that." He agreed that Churchill's view seemed inconsistent with the policy of self-determination and that he was undercutting the Atlantic Charter, saying it was not a rule, just a guide. Roosevelt said:

The Atlantic Charter is a beautiful idea. When it was drawn up, the situation was that England was about to lose the war. They needed hope, and it gave it to them. We have improved the military situation since then at every chance, so that really you might say we have a much better chance of winning the war now than ever before.

The US delegation were still onboard the *Quincy* when Pa Watson died. Churchill cabled: "Accept my deep sympathy in your personal loss through the death of General Watson … I do hope you have benefited by the voyage and will return refreshed."

When they returned home, Roosevelt addressed Congress, while Churchill spoke in the House of Commons. Soon Churchill was bombarding Roosevelt with complaints about Stalin breaking their agreements. In Poland, Stalin was setting up a totalitarian regime before elections were held. He wrote on March 8: "As to the upshot of this, if we do not get things right now, it will soon be seen by the world that you and I by putting our signatures to the Crimea settlement have underwritten a fraudulent prospectus."

There was nothing either of them could do, though Churchill's telegrams became so numerous he had to apologize for them. Roosevelt did not reply. This always worried Churchill. When he heard nothing for two weeks, he wrote again saying: "By the way, did you ever receive a telegram from me of a purely private character … It required no answer. But I should like to know that you received it."

The President had been out of town in Warm Springs, Georgia, and finally did respond: "I did receive your very pleasing message." Then after chit-chat about Clemmie's tour of Russia for the Red Cross, he returned to the business of what to say to Stalin.

PRIME MINISTER'S
PERSONAL TELEGRAM
SERIAL No T.298/5.

PRIME MINISTER TO PRESIDENT
ROOSEVELT No.914.
PERSONAL AND PRIVATE. 18.3.45.

1. I hope that the rather numerous telegrams I have to send you on so many of our difficult and intertwined affairs are not becoming a bore to you. Our friendship is the rock on which I build for the future of the world so long as I am one of the builders. I always think of those tremendous days when you devised Lend-Lease, when we met at Argentia [Newfoundland], when you decided with my heartfelt agreement to launch the invasion of Africa, and when you comforted me for the loss of Tobruk by giving me the 300 Shermans [Sherman tanks] of subsequent Alamein fame. I remember the part our personal relations have played in the advance of the World Cause now nearing its first military goal.

2. I am sending to Washington and San Francisco most of my Ministerial colleagues on one Mission or another, and I shall on this occasion stay at home to mind the shop. All the time I shall be looking forward to your long-promised visit. Clemmie is off to Russia next week for a Red Cross tour as far as the Urals to which she has been invited by Uncle Joe (if we may venture to describe him thus) but she will be back in time to welcome you and Eleanor. My thoughts are always with you all.

3. Peace with Germany and Japan on our terms will not bring much rest to you and me (if I am still responsible). As I observed last time, when the war of the giants is over, the war of the pygmies will begin. There will be a torn, ragged and hungry world to help to its feet; and what will U.J. or his successor say to the way we should both like to do it? It was quite a relief to talk party politics the other day. It was like working in wood after working in steel. The advantage of this telegram is that it has nothing to do with shop except that I had a good talk with Rosenman about our daily bread.

All good wishes,
WINSTON.

GRAVE AND FORMIDABLE DIFFICULTIES

Churchill became concerned that Eisenhower's forces were taking a southerly route in Europe, cutting Germany in two, while leaving the capture of Berlin to the Red Army. Writing as "the truest friends and comrades that ever fought side by side," Churchill insisted: "Berlin remains of high strategic importance. Nothing will exert a psychological effect of despair upon all German forces of resistance equal to that of the fall of Berlin."

But there was another reason that Anglo-American forces should take Berlin, Churchill said:

> The Russian armies will no doubt overrun all Austria and enter Vienna. If they also take Berlin, will not their impression that they have been the overwhelming contributor to our common victory be unduly imprinted in their minds, and may this not lead them into a mood which will raise grave and formidable difficulties in the future?

Roosevelt replied: "It appears reasonable to expect under Eisenhower's present plan the great German Army will in the very near future be completely broken up into separate resistance groups, while our forces will remain tactically intact and in a position to destroy in detail the separated parts of the Nazi Army." The result would be to save as many as one hundred thousand Allied casualties.

Churchill deferred. "I regard the matter as closed," he cabled, "and to prove my sincerity I will use one of my very few Latin quotations, *Amantium irae amoris integratio este*—Lovers' quarrels always go with true love."

ROOSEVELT'S TRIP TO BRITAIN

Roosevelt was still planning ahead for his May trip to Britain. He told Frances Perkins:

> I want to see the British people myself. Eleanor's visit in wartime was a great success. I mean a success for her and for me so that we

American troops entering Munich at the end of the war in 1945.

understood more about their problems. I think they liked her too. But I want to go. We owe it as a return visit, and this seems to be the best time to go. It is going to be all right. I told Eleanor to order her clothes and get some fine ones so that she will make a really handsome appearance.

Sam Rosenman was sent ahead. Discussing the visit with Churchill at Chequers, Rosenman said: "The look which came into Churchill's eyes as he talked showed the strong bond of affection that had grown between these two great leaders."

Churchill then said: "There are two things which I wish you would convey for me to your great President—both matters of personal interest to me."

First, as you know, the President and Mrs. Roosevelt have accepted the invitations of their Majesties to make a visit to England during the month of May. Will you tell him for me that he is going to get from the British people the greatest reception ever accorded to any human being since Lord Nelson made his triumphant return to London? I want you to tell him that when he sees the reception he is going to get, he should realize that it is not an artificial or stimulated one. It will come genuinely and spontaneously from the hearts of the British people; they all love him for what he has done to save them from destruction by the Huns; they love him also for what he has done for the cause of peace in the world, for what he has done to relieve their fear that the horrors they have been through for five years might come upon them again in increased fury.

Rosenman said that Churchill looked a "bit sheepish" when he came to the second matter, and said:

Do you remember when I came over to your country in the summer of 1944 when your election campaigning was beginning? Do you remember that when I arrived, I said something favorable to the election of the President, and immediately the associates of the President sent word to me in no uncertain terms to "lay off" discussing the American election? Do you remember I was told that if I wanted to help the President get re-elected, the best thing I could do was to keep my mouth shut; that the American people would resent any interference or suggestion by a foreigner about how they should vote?

Churchill gave an "engaging laugh" and said:

Now what I want you to tell the President is this. When he comes over here in May I shall be in the midst of a political campaign myself; we shall be holding our own elections about that time. I want you to tell him that I impose no such inhibitions upon him as he imposed upon me. The British people would not resent—and of course I would particularly welcome—any word that he might want to say in favor of my candidacy.

A MESSAGE SO INSULTING

At the time, Roosevelt was resting in Warm Springs, Georgia, comforting himself with a new consignment of gin from London. While the Allies were suspicious of Stalin, he accused them of conducting talks in Bern, Switzerland, over the surrender of German forces in Italy. Roosevelt vehemently denied this and sent a copy of his response to Churchill. This pleased the Prime Minister no-end. It seemed that he and Roosevelt were again united against Stalin, rather than Roosevelt and Stalin ganging up on him, and he wrote to Roosevelt:

I am astounded that Stalin should have addressed to you a message so insulting to the honour of the United States and also of Great Britain. I deem it of the highest importance that a firm and blunt stand should be made at this juncture by our two countries in order that the air may be cleared and they realize that there is a point beyond which we will not tolerate insult. I believe this is the best chance of saving the future. If they are ever convinced that we are afraid of them and can be bullied into submission, then indeed I should despair of our future relations with them and much else.

CLEARLY THE WORK OF OTHERS

The next day he wrote to Clementine, who was still in Russia: "Now that Harry [Hopkins] is ill and Byrnes has resigned, my poor friend is very much alone and, according to all accounts I receive, is bereft of much of his vigour. Many of the telegrams I get from him are clearly the work of others around him."

Indeed, Roosevelt was contemplating retiring in 1946, once the war was over and the United Nations had been set up. Churchill went on to say to Clementine:

> The only times I ever quarrel with the Americans are when they fail to give us a fair share of opportunity to win glory. Undoubtedly I feel much pain when I see our armies so much smaller than theirs. It has always been my wish to keep equal, but how can you do that against so mighty a nation and a population nearly three times your own.

Over a dinner of plovers' eggs and brandy, Jock Colville recorded:

> Talk was of the Americans, the P.M. saying that there was no greater exhibition of power in history than that of the American army fighting the battle of the Ardennes with its left hand and advancing from island to island towards Japan with its right.

THE SULTAN OF MOROCCO

No plovers' eggs and brandy for Roosevelt though. He was reduced to being spoon-fed gruel in an attempt to put on some weight. Lucy Rutherfurd came to visit, and Roosevelt revived enough to mix cocktails and tell tales about Churchill.

"Let's not falter twixt Malta and Yalta," he said, giving a slight garbled version of Churchill's quote. He then related a story about a banquet he said was given for the King of Saudi Arabia, though it was probably the Sultan of Morocco at Casablanca.

"You cannot drink or smoke in his presence, according to Eastern etiquette," he said. "So I called up Winnie to remind him to have his drinks before, which he promptly forgot. At the dinner table, realizing this, he proceeded to sulk through the whole evening, just like this."

He made an imitation of Churchill's expression.

"The idea of the banquet was to exchange friendly bows with the sultan, who controlled great quantities of oil, and surely Churchill's attitude was of no help. At ten o'clock the sultan started to bid farewell. He had hardly left with his entourage when Winnie was already pouring Scotch into a glass!"

WE MUST BE FIRM

While Churchill continued firing off numerous lengthy cables, Roosevelt's output was dwindling to a trickle. On April 11, 1945, he managed two short ones. The first urged caution when dealing with Stalin:

> I would minimize the general Soviet problem as much as possible because these problems, in one form or another, seem to arise every day and most of them straighten out as in the case of the Bern meeting. We must be firm, however, and our course thus far is correct.

The other approved Churchill's proposal to approach the German government, via the Swiss, to get aid to the people of Holland who faced starvation.

That evening Churchill had dinner at the Savoy with Bernard Baruch. "Churchill talked with admiration about the President," Baruch said, "and about Harry Hopkins, of whom he was also very fond."

At 1:15 p.m. on April 12, 1945, Roosevelt was still working when he suffered a cerebral hemorrhage. His doctor was called. The prognosis was not good, so Lucy Rutherfurd, keen to keep her close relationship with Roosevelt a secret to the end, quietly packed and left before the First Lady arrived.

THE YALTA CONFERENCE

The Yalta Conference, also known as the Crimea conference and code named the Argonaut Conference, was held from February 4 to 11, 1945. The meeting was intended mainly to discuss the re-establishment of the nations of war-torn Europe. However within a few short years, with the Cold War dividing the continent, Yalta became a subject of intense controversy. Although Roosevelt and Churchill thought that Stalin was negotiating in good faith, he broke most of the promises he made at Yalta.

The Yalta Conference, Crimea, February 1945. Churchill, Roosevelt, and Stalin photographed in the grounds of the Livadia Palace, Yalta. Standing behind the three leaders are, left to right: British Foreign Secretary Anthony Eden, American Secretary of State Edward Stettinius, British Permanent Under-Secretary of State for Foreign Affairs Sir Alexander Cadogan, the Soviet Commissar for Foreign Affairs Vyacheslav Molotov, and

PART FIVE

EPILOG

Let me assert my firm belief that the only thing we have to fear is fear itself ...
Franklin D. Roosevelt

CHAPTER 18

FDR IS DEAD

President Roosevelt died at 3:35 p.m. on April 12, 1945. When Churchill got the call from Washington giving him the bad news, he said: "I felt as if I had been struck a physical blow."

He cabled Clementine, saying: "I have just heard the grievous news of President Roosevelt's death." And he told Mary: "You know how this will hit me." She said her mother "was stunned by this grievous news. She at once understood its import to the course of events, and knew also what a deep and personal loss the President's death would be to Winston."

Douglas Edwards reporting for CBS from London said:

> *Both King George and Prime Minister Churchill were informed immediately and were deeply shocked and grieved … Britain will always remember President Roosevelt as one of the first men who saw the danger, even before America entered the War. He was the man who sent to these islands the implements with which to fight after the dark days of Dunkirk.*

ONE OF OUR GREATEST FRIENDS

Churchill announced his intention to fly to Washington and received a telegram from Lord Halifax, saying: "Have spoken to Harry Hopkins and Stettinius [Secretary of State Edward Stettinius] who are both much moved by your thought of possibly coming over and who both warmly agree with my judgment of the immense effect for good that would be

President Roosevelt's funeral caisson, April 1945.

Vice-President Harry Truman taking the oath of office on April 12, 1945.

produced … Nor do I overlook the value if you came of your seeing Truman."

A plane was prepared to take him across the Atlantic that night. But first he had more cables to send. To Eleanor Roosevelt, he wrote:

> *Accept my most profound sympathy in your grievous loss, which is also the loss of the British nation and of the cause of freedom in every land. I feel so deeply for you all. As for myself, I have lost a dear and cherished friendship which was forged in the fire of war. I trust you may find consolation in the magnitude of his work and the glory of his name.*

And he wrote to Harry Hopkins:

> *I understand how deep your feelings of grief must be. I feel with you that we have lost one of our greatest friends and one of the most valiant champions of the causes for which we fight. I feel a very painful personal loss, quite apart from the ties of public action which bound us so closely together. I had a true affection for Franklin.*

THE GRIEVOUS NEWS

Churchill had never met Harry S. Truman, now 33rd President of the United States. Nevertheless he cabled the new President:

> *Pray accept from me the expression of my personal sympathy in the loss which you and the American nation have sustained in the death of our illustrious friend. I hope that I may be privileged to renew with you the intimate comradeship in the great cause we all serve that I enjoyed through these terrible years with him. I offer you my respectful good wishes as you step into the breach in the victorious lines of the United Nations.*

Truman responded:

> *At no time in our respective histories, has it been more important that the intimate, solid relations which you and the late President had forged between our countries be preserved and developed. It is my earnest hope that before too long, in the furtherance of this, we can arrange a personal meeting … You can count on me to continue the loyal and close*

collaboration which to the benefit of the entire world existed between you and our great President.

Churchill went to the House of Commons to break the grievous news, telling the members:

The House will have learned with deepest sorrow the grievous news which has come to us from across the Atlantic and which conveys to us the loss of a famous President of the United States, whose friendship for the cause of freedom and for the causes of the weak and poor have won him immortal renown. It is not fitting that we should continue our work this day. I feel that the House will wish to render its token of respect to the memory of this great departed statesman and war leader by adjourning immediately.

Quite apart from his public face, in private Churchill was devastated, saying:

I feel a very painful personal loss, quite apart from the ties of public action which bound us so closely together.

THE REPRIEVE OF CIVILIZATION

On April 13, 1945, London's *News Chronicle* reported:

As for the British people, FDR must always hold, so long as our nation lasts, a place in our affections and our gratitude as few foreigners if any have held in our history. He foresaw the peril and determined that his country should meet it with all her strength. But while he was mobilizing home opinion and planning the development of the immense resources of the American nation, he did not hesitate by one act after another to give priceless aid to Britain as she fought alone.

The sending of rifles when France fell, the destroyers and the bases, the repeal of the Neutrality Act and finally the supreme generosity of Lend-Lease—history may perhaps be able to assess just how much these priceless and courageous gestures contributed towards the saving of Britain's freedom and the reprieve of civilization.

A LETTER FROM THE KING

Churchill received a letter of condolence himself. In a handwritten note, King George VI said:

I cannot tell you how sad I am at the sudden death of President Roosevelt. The news came as a great shock to me. I have lost a friend, but to you who have known him for so long and so intimately during this war, the sudden loss to yourself personally of a colleague & helpmate in the framing of far reaching decisions both for the prosecution of the war and for the future peace of the world must be overwhelming. I send you all my sympathy at this moment.

Churchill replied:

I am touched by the kindness of Your Majesty's letter. The sudden loss of this great friend and comrade in all our affairs is very hard for me. Ties have been shorn asunder which years had woven. We have to begin again in many ways. I was tempted during the day to go over for the funeral and begin relations with the new man. However so many of Your Majesty's Ministers are out of the country, and the Foreign Secretary had arranged to go anyhow, and I felt the business next week in Parliament and also the ceremonies connected with the death of Mr. Roosevelt are so important that I should be failing in my duty if I left the House of Commons without my close personal attention. I had to consider the tribute which should be paid to the late President, which clearly it is my business to deliver. The press of work is also very heavy. Therefore I thought it better that I should remain here in charge at this juncture …

Moreover I think that it would be a good thing that President Truman should come over here at about the same time as was proposed by his predecessor. He could visit his Armies in Germany, and he could be Your Majesty's guest.

THE COST OF INVADING JAPAN

In the end, Churchill did not fly to Washington that night as planned, though he later regretted it. He told Harry Hopkins: "It would have been a solace to me to be present at Franklin's funeral, but everyone here thought my duty next week lay at home, at a time when so many Ministers are out of the country."

The Associated Press announced: "Prime Minister Churchill wanted to come but was too busy." Having been vice president for just seventy-three days before stepping into Roosevelt's shoes, Truman was much too busy learning the top job to travel, so he could not come to England as Churchill had hoped.

Within twenty-four hours of President Roosevelt's death, President Truman was told about the Manhattan Project by Secretary of War, Henry Stimson. He was also reading military assessments which predicted the invasion of Japan, now scheduled for 1946, would cost as many as a million casualties, given the use of kamikazes and the suicidal defense of Iwo Jima and Okinawa.

Churchill was seen weeping at a memorial service held in St. Paul's Cathedral. Taking a leaf out of Churchill's book, the dean praised the dead President: "We who represent the two great English-speaking peoples are specially bound to pray that through our cooperation one with another the great causes for which Franklin Delano Roosevelt labored may be brought to fruition for the lasting benefit of all the nations of the world."

Winston Churchill with his daughter Sarah, leaving the memorial service held for President Roosevelt at St. Paul's Cathedral, London, April 17, 1945.

Franklin D. Roosevelt did not live to see the end of the war that he had fought so hard to win, he died in April 1945, just 11 weeks into his fourth term. The Axis Powers surrendered to the Allies in the months following Roosevelt's death.

THE GREATEST CHAMPION OF FREEDOM

Excerpt from Churchill's Tribute to President Roosevelt

April 17, 1945, House of Commons

My friendship with the great man to whose work and fame we pay our tribute today began and ripened during this war. I had met him, but only for a few minutes, after the close of the last war, and as soon as I went to the Admiralty in September 1939, he telegraphed, inviting me to correspond with him direct on naval or other matters if at any time I felt inclined …

When I became Prime Minister, and the war broke out in all its hideous fury, when our own life and survival hung in the balance, I was already in a position to telegraph to the President on terms of an association which had become most intimate and, to me most agreeable. This continued through all the ups and downs of the world struggle until Thursday last, when I received my last messages from him …

I conceived an admiration for him as a statesman, a man of affairs, and a war leader. I felt the utmost confidence in his upright, inspiring character and outlook, and a personal regard and affection—I must say—for him beyond my power to express today. His love of his own country, his respect for its constitution, his power of gauging the tides and currents of its mobile public opinion, were always evident, but added to these were the beatings of that generous heart which was always stirred to anger and to action by spectacles of aggression and oppression by the strong against the weak. It is, indeed, a loss—a bitter loss to humanity—that those heart-beats are stilled for ever …

There is no doubt that the President foresaw the great dangers closing in upon the prewar world with far more prescience than most well-informed people on either side of the Atlantic, and that he urged forward with all his power such precautionary military preparations as peace-time opinion in the United States could be brought to accept. There never was a moment's doubt, as the quarrel opened, upon which side his sympathies lay. The fall of France, and what seemed to most people outside this Island the impending destruction of Great Britain, were to him an agony although he never lost faith in us. They were an agony to him not only on account of Europe, but because of the serious perils to which the United States herself would have been exposed had we been overwhelmed or the survivors cast down under the German yoke …

He devised the extraordinary measure of assistance called Lend-Lease, which will stand forth as the most unselfish and unsordid financial act of any country in all history. The effect of this was greatly to increase British fighting power, and for all the purposes of the war effort to make us, as it were, a much more numerous community … All this time, in deep and dark and deadly secrecy, the Japanese were preparing their act of treachery and greed. When next we met in Washington, Japan, Germany, and Italy had declared war upon the United States, and both our countries were in arms, shoulder to shoulder. Since then we have advanced over the land and over the sea through many difficulties and disappointments, but always with a broadening measure of success …

When I took my leave of him in Alexandria harbor I must confess that I had an indefinable sense of fear that his health and his strength were on the ebb. But nothing altered his inflexible sense of duty. To the end he faced his innumerable tasks unflinching … When death came suddenly upon him "he had finished his mail." That portion of his day's work was done. As the saying goes, he died in harness, and we may well say in battle harness, like his soldiers, sailors, and airmen, who side by side with ours are carrying on their task to the end all over the world. What an enviable death was his! He had brought his country through the worst of its perils and the heaviest of its toils. Victory had cast its sure and steady beam upon him. In the days of peace he had broadened and stabilized the foundations of American life and union. In war he had raised the strength, might and glory of the great Republic to a height never attained by any nation in history …

For us, it remains only to say that in Franklin Roosevelt there died the greatest American friend we have ever known, and the greatest champion of freedom who has ever brought help and comfort from the new world to the old.

THE POTSDAM CONFERENCE

By the time Roosevelt died, the war in Europe had been won. The Nazi concentration and death camps were opened, once again underscoring the moral purpose of the war. Hitler shot himself in his bunker in Berlin on April 30, and Germany surrendered on May 7, 1945.

Truman and Churchill flew to Germany to meet Stalin at the Potsdam Conference, which opened on July 17. The previous day, the first atomic bomb had been detonated in the deserts of New Mexico. Truman told Stalin that the US had a "new weapon."

Churchill returned to England on July 25 for the general election the following day. He was voted out of office and was replaced at the Potsdam Conference by the new Prime Minister Clement Attlee. On July 26, an ultimatum was sent to Tokyo, demanding Japan's unconditional surrender and threatening a step-up in the bombing campaign.

Japan refused to surrender, so on August 6, 1945, an atomic bomb was dropped on the city of Hiroshima, killing between 70,000 and 80,000 people and injuring over 70,000 others. When this too did not prompt a surrender, a second bomb was dropped on Nagasaki on August 9, killing between 35,000 and 40,000 more people. The following day, Japan finally capitulated.

Churchill and Clementine traveled to the United States and visited Roosevelt's grave at Hyde Park on March 12, 1946, with Eleanor who wrote:

I think it was a day of great emotion for Mr. Churchill. Besides the respect he had for my husband as a statesman, which made it possible for them to work together even when they differed, he also had a real affection for him as a human being, just as my husband had for him.

Winston Churchill, Harry Truman, and Joseph Stalin at the Potsdam Conference, July 1945. During the conference, Churchill lost a general election and Clement Attlee became Britain's new prime minister and representative at the conference.

AN IRON CURTAIN HAS DESCENDED

A week earlier, alongside President Truman, Churchill had made a speech at Westminster College in Fulton, Missouri, saying: "From Stettin in the Baltic to Trieste in the Adriatic, an iron curtain has descended across the continent." This speech was thought to mark the beginning of the Cold War.

Then Eleanor Roosevelt visited London again in 1948:

My husband had looked forward to the joy of sharing with Mr. Churchill the gratitude of the people of England. But just as Moses was shown the promised land and could not enter, I imagine there are many men who see their hopes and plans developing but who are never actually allowed to have on this earth the recognition they might well have enjoyed.

Churchill became prime minister again in October 1951. He survived a stroke in July 1953, but with his powers failing he resigned on April 5, 1955. In 1963, he was the first foreign national to be granted honorary US citizenship. At age 91, he died on January 24, 1965, having survived Roosevelt, who was eight years younger, by nearly twenty years.

Churchill raises his hat to the crowd during his farewell tour of London, after losing the election in July 1945.

A PHILOSOPHER'S VIEWPOINT

Russian-born philosopher Isaiah Berlin was an information officer in the British Embassy, Washington DC, during World War II, and gave his assessment of the relationship between Churchill and Roosevelt:

Each appeared to the other in a romantic light high above the battles of allies or subordinates: their meetings and correspondence were occasions to which both consciously rose; they were royal cousins and felt pride in this relationship, tempered by a sharp and sometimes amused, but never ironical, perception of the other's peculiar qualities. The relationship born during the great historical upheaval, somewhat aggrandized by its solemnity, never flagged or degenerated, but retained a combination of formal dignity and exuberant high spirits which can scarcely ever before have bound the heads of states. Each was personally fascinated not so much by the other as by the idea of the other, and infected him by his own peculiar brand of high spirits …

The relationship was made genuine by something more than even the solid community of interest or personal and official respect or admiration—namely, by the peculiar degree to which they liked each other's delight in the oddities and humors of life and their own active part in it. This was a unique personal bond, which Harry Hopkins understood and encouraged to the fullest degree. Mr. Roosevelt's sense of fun was perhaps the lighter, Mr. Churchill's a trifle grimmer.

Early in 1944, Churchill heard Berlin was in London and invited him to lunch. "When do you think the war will end, Mr. Berlin?" he asked, only to discover his guest was not Isaiah Berlin, but one of America's greatest songwriters Irving Berlin, composer of *God Bless America* and *White Christmas*.

Isaiah Berlin.

Irving Berlin.

SIR WINSTON CHURCHILL'S FUNERAL

The planning for "Operation Hope Not," the code name for the funeral arrangements of Sir Winston Churchill, began in the late 1950s. Such was the scale and significance of the event that meticulous and timely preparations were essential. Their implementation came on a gray Saturday morning in January 1965, four days after the death of the great wartime leader. The plans included provision for an extraordinary procession through London, a ceremony at St. Paul's Cathedral, dispatch of the coffin from the Tower of London by river launch, a military fly past, and a train from Waterloo Station to Churchill's burial place at St. Martin's Church in Bladon, Oxfordshire; arrangements requiring the kind of military precision that would have pleased Churchill himself no-end. In one of the most poignant moments of modern British history—all the dockland construction cranes dipped in silent tribute as Churchill's coffin passed down the River Thames.

Winston Churchill's funeral procession through central London, January 30, 1965.

I shall never cease to be grateful to Churchill for his leadership during the war. The real affection which he had for my husband and which was reciprocated, he has apparently never lost. The war would have been harder to win without it, and the two men might not have gone through it so well if they had not had that personal pleasure in meeting and confidence in each other's integrity and ability.

Eleanor Roosevelt

FURTHER READING

This book documents the friendship between President Franklin D. Roosevelt and Prime Minister Winston Churchill, and is designed to be an informative and entertaining introductory text. There are many more academic publications available should the reader wish to delve more deeply. Publications that were especially useful during the preparation of this book are listed below, and other credits are cited at the point where they appear within the text.

Alldritt, Keith, *The Greatest of Friends: Franklin D. Roosevelt and Winston Churchill 1941 – 1945*. St Martin's Press, 1995.

Black, Conrad, *Franklin Delano Roosevelt*. Public Affairs, 2005.

Brooke, Alan Francis, *Alanbrooke War Diaries 1939 – 1945: Field Marshall Lord Alanbrooke*. Weidenfeld & Nicolson, 2002.

Churchill, Winston, *Great Contemporaries: Churchill Reflects on FDR, Hitler, Kipling, Chaplin, Balfour, and Other Giants of His Age*. ISI Books , 2012.

Churchill, Winston, *The Second World War. History WWII 6 vols.* Houghton Mifflin,1948 – 1953. 1953 Nobel Prize in Literature

Churchwell, Sarah, *Behold America: A History of America First and the American Dream*. Bloomsbury, 2018.

Colville, John Rupert, *The Fringes Of Power. 10 Downing Street Diaries 1939 – 1955*. W.W. Norton, 1989.

Edward Smith, Jean, *FDR*. Random House, 2008.

Gilbert, Martin, *Churchill: A Life*. Holt Paperbacks, 1992.

Goodwin, Doris Kearns, *No Ordinary Time: Franklin and Eleanor Roosevelt - The Home Front in World War II*. Simon & Schuster, 1995.

Hamilton, Nigel, *The Mantle of Command: FDR at War, 1941 – 1942*. Houghton Mifflin, 2014.

Hamilton, Nigel, *Commander in Chief: FDR's Battle with Churchill. FDR at War, 1943*. Biteback, 2016.

Jackson, Robert H., *That Man: An Insider's Portrait of Franklin D. Roosevelt*. Oxford University Press, 2004.

Jenkins, Roy, *Churchill: A Biography*. Pan, 2002.

Kimball, Warren F., *Churchill and Roosevelt: The Complete Correspondence* (3 Volumes) Princeton University Press, 1984.

Kimball, Warren F., *Forged in War: Roosevelt, Churchill, and the Second World War*. Ivan R. Dee, 2002.

Lash, Joseph P., *Roosevelt and Churchill: The Partnership That Saved the West, 1939 – 1941*. W.W. Norton, 1980.

Lehrman, Lewis, *Churchill, Roosevelt, and Company*. Stackpole Books, 2017.

Manchester, William, *The Last Lion: Winston Spencer Churchill: Defender of the Realm, 1940 – 1965*. Bantam, 2013.

McCarten, Anthony, *Darkest Hour: Official Tie-In for the Oscar-Winning Film Starring Gary Oldman*. Viking 2017.

McElvaine, Robert S., *Franklin Delano Roosevelt (American Press Reference Series)*. CQ Press, 2002.

McMoran Wilson, Charles, *Winston Churchill. The struggle for survival, 1940 – 1965, Taken from the diaries of Lord Moran*. Constable, 1966.

Meacham, Jon, *Franklin and Winston: An Intimate Portrait of an Epic Friendship*. Random House, 2004.

Morton Blum, John (ed), *The Price of Vision: The Diary of Henry A. Wallace 1942 – 1946*. Houghton Mifflin, 1973.

Pendar, Kenneth, *Adventure in Diplomacy: The Emergence of General de Gaulle in North Africa*. Casey, 1966.

Sainsbury, Keith, *Churchill and Roosevelt At War: The War They Fought and the Peace They Hoped to Make*. NYU Press, 1994.

Stafford, David, *Roosevelt and Churchill: Men of Secrets*. Thistle Publishing, 2013.

United States Holocaust Memorial Museum, *A Forgotten Suitcase: The Mantello Rescue Mission*. www.ushmm.org.

Winik, Jay, *1944: FDR and the Year That Changed History*. Simon & Schuster, 2016.

World Jewish Congress, *Unity in Dispersion A History of the World Jewish Congress*. World Jewish Congress, 1948.

Wyman, David S., *Abandonment of the Jews: America and the Holocaust, 1941 – 45*. Pantheon Books Inc, 1984.

ATORS
THE
RLD

LUXEMBURG

NETHERLANDS

NORWAY

YUGOSLAVIA

GREECE

RUSSIA

An American World War II poster showing portraits of
Roosevelt and Churchill, with flags of the Allies and
the sinking of the Japanese battleship *Haruna*.

INDEX

Page numbers in italic denote an illustration

© 2018 Oxford Publishing Ventures Ltd

This edition published in 2018 by Chartwell Books,
an imprint of The Quarto Group,
142 West 36th Street, 4th Floor,
New York, NY 10018, USA
T (212) 779-4972 **F** (212) 779-6058
www.QuartoKnows.com

10 9 8 7 6 5 4 3 2 1

ISBN: 978-0-7858-3633-9

Printed in China

PICTURE CREDITS

The publishers are grateful to the Franklin D. Roosevelt Presidential Library and Museum (FDRPLM) for the supply of images. Some images are released from the Library of Congress Prints and Photographs Division (loc.gov), as works of the US federal government these images are in the public domain. Others are from the public archives of the Imperial War Museum in London (IWM). The images listed below are all in the public domain unless otherwise stated.

Cover images: loc.gov / Heritage Image Partnership Ltd / Pictorial Press Ltd / Photo 12 / Everett Collection Inc / Alamy

Internal images: 2 FDRPLM / 4 Ullstein bild Dtl. / Getty / 6 loc.gov / 7 IWM / 8 Hulton Deutsch / Getty / 11 Everett Collection Inc / Alamy / 12 George Skadding / The Life Picture Collection / Getty / 13 Carl Mydans / The Life Picture Collection / Getty / 14 Granger Historical Picture Archive / Alamy / 16 Granger Historical Picture Archive / Alamy / 19 Everett Collection Inc / Alamy / 21 World History Archive / Alamy / 23 Hi-Story / Alamy / 24 Bettmann / 25 Marka / Alamy / 26 FDRPLM / 29 Pach Bros., NYC, 1904 / 30 Endicott Peabody / 31 GL Archive / Alamy / 32 FDRPLM / 33 Heritage Image Partnership Ltd / Alamy / 34 William Barnes Wollen 1899 / 35 Military History Collection / Alamy / 36 Pictorial Press Ltd / Alamy / 38 Chronicle / Alamy / 40 Fremantle / Alamy / 44 Interfoto / Alamy / 45 Strand Magazine 1935 / 46 Pictorial Press Ltd / Alamy / 48 Shawshots / Alamy / 49 Lordprice Collection / Alamy / 50 Keystone Pictures USA / Alamy / 52 Ullstein bild Dtl. / Getty / 57 Yousuf Karsh, 1941 / 59 ilduce.net / 63 Granger Historical Picture Archive / Alamy / 64 Everett Collection Inc / Alamy / 65 12 / UIG / Getty / 67 World History Archive / Alamy / 68 Bettmann / Getty / 70 Everett Collection Inc / Alamy / 72 loc.gov/ 73 Wide World Photos / 76 loc.gov / 77 charleslindbergh.com / 78 Popperfoto / Getty / 80 Keystone Pictures USA / Alamy / 82 Pictorial Press Ltd / Alamy / 84 Gino Boccasile 1941 / 86 Military History Collection / Alamy / 89 Pictorial Press Ltd / Alamy / 90 Bettmann/ Getty / 93 FDRPLM / 95 Bettmann/ Getty / 96 FDRPLM / 97 Atomic / Alamy / 99 Granger Historical Picture Archive / Alamy / 100 Interfoto / Alamy / 102 Lordprice Collection / Alamy / 104 Granger Historical Picture Archive / Alamy / 105 IWM / 107 World History Archive / Alamy / 109 Time Life Pictures/ Getty / 111 Everett Collection Inc / Alamy / 114 Macarena Bohorquez Capilla / Alamy / 115 christies.com / 116 Everett Collection Inc / Alamy / 118 Everett Collection Historical / Alamy / 120 Peter Stackpole / The Life Picture Collection/Getty / 121 Library of Congress / Corbis/VCG / Getty Images / 122 Everett Collection Inc / Alamy Stock Photo / 124 Pictorial Press Ltd / Alamy / 125 Dmitri Kessel / The Life Premium Collection/Getty / 127 FDRPLM / 128 Heritage Image Partnership Ltd / Alamy / 130 Ken Hawkins / Alamy / 132 FDRPLM / 134 Paul Popper/Popperfoto / Getty / 135 Keystone / Getty / 136 Everett Collection Historical / Alamy / 138 Everett Collection Historical / Alamy / 141 Bettmann / Getty / 142 Everett Collection Historical / Alamy / 144 ClassicStock / Alamy / 145 Photo 12 / Alamy / 146 Military History Collection / Alamy / 147 Bettmann / Getty / 150 Time Life Pictures / US Army / The Life Picture Collection / Getty / 153 DPA picture alliance / Alamy / 156 Galerie Bilderwelt / Getty / 158 FDRPLM / 160 Moses Parker Rice 1863 / 161 FDRPLM / 163 Photo 12 / Alamy / 167 Interfoto / Alamy / 170 IWM / 172, 174, 175 Everett Collection Historical / Alamy / 177 Dave Bagnall Collection / Alamy / 178 FDRPLM / 180 Everett Collection Historical / Alamy / 181 Topical Press Agency/Getty / 182L Geoff A Howard / Alamy / 182R Everett Collection Historical / Alamy / 183 Marka / Alamy / 184 FDRPLM / 186 The Frent Collection / Corbis / Getty